PAPER
in three dimensions

PAPER
in three dimensions
Origami, Pop-ups, Sculpture, Baskets, Boxes, and More

DIANE MAURER-MATHISON

WATSON-GUPTILL PUBLICATIONS/NEW YORK

TO THE MEMORY OF HAL LOSE,
AN EXTRAORDINARY PAPER SCULPTOR AND FRIEND

ACKNOWLEDGMENTS
Sincere thanks to all the paper artists whose inspiring works fill this book.

ARTIST COPYRIGHT
The designs, patterns, and projects in this book are intended for the personal use of
the reader only. Any other use is forbidden under law without written permission of
the artists/copyright holders. The addresses of artists whose work appears in this
book are included in the list of contributors on page 127.
Note: All line art, unless otherwise credited below, is by Jeffery Mathison.
© Ingrid Siliakus, diagram on page 72.
© Sandy Jackson, diagram on page 78.

First published in 2006 by Watson-Guptill Publications,
a division of VNU Business Media, Inc.,
770 Broadway, New York, NY 10003
www.wgpub.com

ISBN-13: 978-0-8230-6778-7
ISBN: 0-8230-6778-5

Library of Congress Control Number: 2005937222

Senior Editor: Joy Aquilino
Editor: Holly Jennings
Designer: Areta Buk/Thumb Print
Production Manager: Hector Campbell

Printed in China

First printing 2006

1 2 3 4 5 6 7 8 9 / 14 13 12 11 10 09 08 07 06

Text set in 11-pt. Adobe Garamond

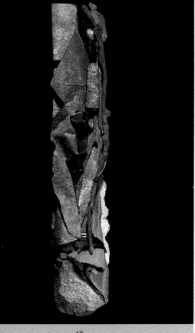

Contents

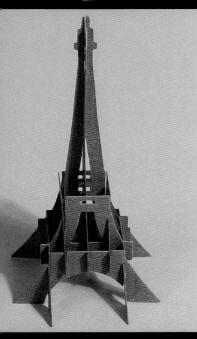

IT IS HARD TO IMAGINE a more versatile medium for any artist or craftsperson to work in than paper. Sheets of the inexpensive material we use every day can be folded and twisted, bent and curled, woven, slit, stitched, layered, collaged, wrapped, embossed, and manipulated in myriad ways to create fine craft and artworks. Even more possibilities are presented when you make your own paper. Paper pulp can be sprayed over armatures, poured over objects, pressed into various types of molds, and used as a dimensional painting medium.

Paper's long history as a sacred and mystical material continues in Japan and many other parts of the world today. Paper has the power to entrance, amuse, and amaze, whether it is presented as a pop-up card, paper mask, three-dimensional book or paper sculpture.

Because dimensional paper is so eye-catching, it also acts as a perfect vehicle for communication. Traditional paper sculpture has been used by graphic artists and illustrators to advertise products both in store window displays and in print for decades. Paper sculptor Hal Lose, whose work has won international design awards, has created many pieces specifically for advertising art. Most of us have already dabbled in paper sculpture and unknowingly used it to advertise and communicate our feelings. Consider the pile of paper torn to shreds over an unwelcome piece of mail, the tightly crumpled ball of paper indicative of another computer printer error, or the twisted napkin that might remain after a difficult holiday dinner. I once left a fleet of tiny paper airplanes behind when I exited a boring meeting, but then I suspected they might convey a message.

Paper in Three Dimensions will show you how to move beyond your unconscious forays into paper sculpture, to transform your own handmade or purchased paper into exciting dimensional paper art. We'll explore low relief embossed and cast paper as well as three-dimensional paper "in the round." Some of the projects presented, like a pop-up flag book or origami bowl, will be quite easy to create while others, like the sculptural woven basket or Architectural Canal House, will require a bit more time to complete. Basic techniques for making and working with paper are presented at the beginning of the book for people with limited experience in paper art.

Many of the paper artists whose works are shown in this book, are teachers, authors and leaders in their fields. The tips and techniques they present in photographic visits to their studios will help you quickly navigate the various paper art media. The work that they present in the gallery section that follows each chapter will inspire you to create your own exciting and unique designs.

BELOW *FEATHERED NEST*
(5^1/$_4$ × 2^3/$_4$ × 1 INCHES, CLOSED)
BY ANNE-CLAUDE COTTY
OPPOSITE *ETHIOPIAN SPIRIT OF THE TIMES* (46 × 18 × 6 INCHES)
BY DANIEL ESSIG

CHAPTER 1

Creating
DIMENSIONAL HANDMADE PAPER

DIMENSIONAL HANDMADE PAPER structures can be created in virtually any size or shape, from a tiny circular brooch to a massive wall piece whose size belies its light weight. Some works, like those by Marjorie Tomchuk, conform to the height of their embossing plate and are classified as low-relief dimensional handmade paper, while others, like Barbara Fletcher's animals made of pulp cast into plaster molds, can become fully three-dimensional. Because paper pulp is lightweight and flexible, in the hands of an artist such as Jeanne Petrosky, it can also become a fine paper sculpting material, and produce a work not bound by the size or shape of plates or molds used to create it.

Many dimensional handmade paper structures are created by rewetting and pressing a previously made sheet of handmade paper into a mold or over a base or armature. Although you can purchase sheets of handmade paper, rewet them, and proceed, it is great fun to start from scratch and make your own paper. You'll be amazed at how easy it is.

OPPOSITE *OVERGROWN, MIXED MEDIA CAST PAPER BY LESLIE EBERT*
Leslie works with wet pulp and casts it on top of a carved block to deeply emboss her handmade paper works.

Basic Papermaking

EQUIPMENT AND MATERIALS

Inexpensive papermaking kits with molds, deckles, felts, and linters (pulp in sheet form) are sold in most large art and craft shops and through papermaking suppliers. Or you can improvise by making some of the equipment and also using household items you may have on hand. As your interest in papermaking grows, you may want to invest in more expensive equipment and purchase a book on papermaking to explore the craft more fully, but the basic papermaking skills described here will get you started creating exciting dimensional paper art.

COUCHING CLOTHS OR FELTS These are used to support newly formed sheets of paper, separate sheets in a post of papers, and draw water from them as they are pressed. The term *felt* is usually used by papermakers to refer to any couching material. You can purchase new felts from a papermaking supplier or cut apart old army blankets. Nonfusible interfacing from a fabric store or old cotton sheets can also be used to support newly formed sheets of paper. Felts should be about 2 inches larger all around than the paper you intend to make. Handi Wipes can also be used if you don't mind the slight pattern they impart to the papers. Papermaker Leslie Ebert often searches for highly textured couching cloths to give unusual patterns to her handmade paper.

KITCHEN BLENDER You'll need a basic blender for macerating the fiber to make the paper pulp. Purchase one to use for papermaking only.

LARGE DISHPAN OR PLASTIC STORAGE CONTAINER Either of these can serve as a papermaking vat. The vat should be about 7 inches deep and large enough to accommodate the mold and deckle and your hands, with room to spare.

LARGE FLAT BRUSH This will help transfer the pressed sheet of paper to a Plexiglas drying surface.

MOLD AND DECKLE The mold is the screened frame on which the newly formed sheet of paper rests. The deckle, which resembles a picture frame, sits on top of the mold to keep the pulp in place. The mold and matching deckle determine the size and shape of the sheet of paper made. Purchase a mold and deckle through a papermaking supplier or through an art supply store or catalog. They are inexpensive and readily available.

PIGMENTS AND RETENTION AID For vibrant permanently colored papers, order pigments and retention aid (to help the pigments bond to the paper fibers) from a papermaking supplier. Follow the instructions from the supplier for using them. You can also add colored papers or try using fabric dyes to color your pulp.

PRESSING BOARDS You'll need two of these made from Formica or from urethaned wood. They should be slightly larger than your paper mold. These will sandwich your post or stack of couched sheets and, with the help of some weight placed atop them, remove most of the water from your newly formed sheets of paper. A simple paper press made with C-clamps or from bolts and wood, like the one shown in the diagram on the opposite page, is an efficient way to press a stack of wet paper. Or you can purchase a nifty paper press from a papermaking supply house or large art supply store.

RECYCLED PAPER Computer paper, photocopy paper, old blotters, and pieces of drawing paper and mount board can all be used to make handmade paper. Newspapers and magazines should be avoided as they are highly acidic. If you are concerned with producing papers that are archival (and aren't peppered with tiny letters) be diligent about what you use. To produce papers that are archival, you should use recycled papers that are as close to pH neutral (neither acidic nor alkaline) as possible. Lineco makes a pH-testing pen that you can use to determine the pH of papers in question. Most should have a pH of 6.5 or higher.

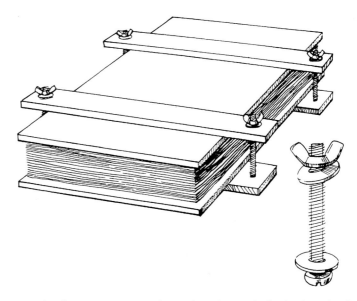

SHEET OF PLEXIGLAS OR FORMICA Either will make a good surface for paper drying. They will also impart a smooth surface to one side of your handmade paper. Plexiglas is also useful for special paper sculpting and pulp painting techniques, like those used by Jeanne Petrosky for her rock sculptures (see page 20) and Betsy Miraglia for her dimensional pulp painting (see page 30).

SHEETS OF PULP Pulp made from abaca (banana leaf fibers) or cotton linters can be ordered in sheet form from papermaking supply houses. These sheets of pulp are easy to use and produce fine papers. Many suppliers also sell buckets of pulp if you want to skip the pulping process altogether.

SIZING Liquid sizing, available from a papermaking supplier, can be added to your pulp to make sheets less absorbent and more receptive to lettering with calligraphy inks.

SPONGES These will be used for clean up, releasing ornery sheets from the mold, and pressing excess water out of newly couched or cast paper. They can also be used for rewetting dry sheets that are to be embossed.

To create a simple paper press, cut four strips of 1-x-4-inch pine board at least 6 inches longer than your urethaned pressboards. Drill 3/8-inch holes about 1 1/2 inches in from either end of each strip and insert long carriage bolts (1/4-inch diameter) through the holes to sandwich the stack of wet papers and pressboards. Add washers and wing nuts to the bolts and twist them to tighten the press.

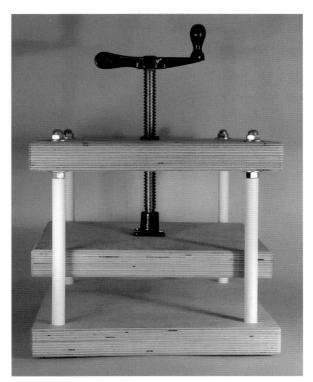

A ready-made commercial paper press, like this one made by Arnold Grummer, makes pressing papers easy.

STRAINER AND MESH CURTAIN You can use these to strain out the extra pulp at the end of your papermaking session and store it for later use.

WATER Sometimes mineral or organic compounds in water will cause brown stains to appear in a dried sheet of paper. To be on the safe side, I use purified or distilled water for papermaking.

BASIC TECHNIQUES

The basic papermaking process involves dipping a screened frame and its companion deckle into a vat of floating paper pulp, scooping some of the pulp up as you lift the mold and deckle out of the vat, and then shaking the screen side to side and back and forth to help the paper fibers interlock as the water drains from them. The newly formed paper is then couched or transferred from the mold to a sheet of Plexiglas, for some projects like pulp painting, or to dampened cloth or felt to help support the sheet and draw water from it. After the sheet is covered with another cloth and pressed between boards, it can be used to make a cast paper work or an embossing, or dried to later become part a dimensional handmade paper project.

Lowering the mold and deckle into a vat to make a sheet of paper.

MAKING PAPER IN A HOME BLENDER

Various types of drawing papers and office stock can be recycled to make paper, but it is easiest to begin making paper in a home blender by purchasing linters. To make paper from linters, wet several linters and tear them into 1-inch pieces. Add a small handful of torn linters to a blender two-thirds full of warm water. (A general rule is to use about one part linters to two parts warm water.) Beat for about one minute, using short bursts of speed to avoid straining the blender motor.

Empty the blended pulp into your papermaking vat and add about two more blenderfuls of water. Continue beating and pouring into your vat, adding additional water each time, until you have about 1 pint concentrated pulp mixed with 4 gallons of water. You needn't be too concerned with exact proportions. The ratio of pulp to water can be adjusted to create thinner or thicker sheets by adding more water or concentrated pulp to your vat.

USING A MOLD AND DECKLE TO FORM A SHEET

To make a sheet of paper, use your hand to stir and distribute the pulp throughout the water in your vat. Place your deckle on top of the screened side of your mold so that the flat edges are together. Hold the deckle in place with your thumbs and grasp the mold underneath with your fingers. If your mold is rectangular, place your hands in position on the short sides.

Hold the mold and deckle at a slight angle and lower them into the vat at the far edge. Then bring the mold and deckle toward you, shifting them to a horizontal position. Hold them level for a moment just below the water's surface before lifting them swiftly up and out of the vat.

As the water drains through the screen, gently shake the mold and deckle from side to side and from front to back to disperse and mesh the pulp fibers you've scooped up.

When most of the water has drained back into the vat, tilt the mold and deckle slightly to let additional excess water drain off. Now rest your mold and deckle on the edge of the vat and carefully remove the deckle.

COUCHING

After you've removed the deckle from the mold it's time to couch (rhymes with *pooch*) the sheet. The term comes from the French, meaning "to lay down," and refers to transferring the newly formed sheet of paper to the dampened cloth or felt. If you aren't planning to couch your newly formed paper onto a carved plate or into a mold, you'll need to prepare a couching pad by placing a dampened felt on a urethaned pressboard and placing another dampened piece of cotton fabric or interfacing on top of the felt. Smooth out any wrinkles in the cloths (unless you want the wrinkles to remain and add texture to the sheet) and then stand your mold upright at the edge of the cloth and roll the mold firmly down. When the opposite edge of the mold makes contact with the cloth, lift the first edge up. Usually the slight rocking motion releases the sheet of paper. (If you have difficulty getting the paper to let go at first, place the mold facedown on the couching cloth and use a wet sponge to press out some of the moisture and release the back of the sheet through the mold screen.) At this point your paper is ready for sheet casting, described on page 22. If you'd rather build up a stack, or "post," of papers to dry for later use, continue couching and adding dampened cloths until you've created a stack of about ten sheets. Then add another thick felt and cover with a pressboard.

PRESSING

If you don't want to invest in a professional paper press, you can place C-clamps on the pressboards sandwiching your stack of papers and tighten them to press out as much moisture as you can. A simple press using bolts going through the pressboards

Couching the newly made sheet of paper.

and wing nuts to force the boards together would also function well (see diagram on page 11). If you're pressing indoors, be sure to elevate the post of papers in a tub or kitty litter pan to allow the water to drain without flooding your home or studio.

DRYING

When most of the moisture has been pressed out of your handmade paper, you can brush the back of your couching sheet to transfer your paper to Plexiglas or you can pin each couching cloth, with damp sheet attached, to Styrofoam or urethaned wood to minimize shrinkage, and let the sheets air dry. Sheets can then be stored and rewetted for specific three-dimensional paper projects.

CLEANING UP

Use a strainer or mesh fabric to strain out any pulp that's left in your vat after papermaking before pouring the liquid down the drain. If you have a quantity of pulp left over, you can compress it into balls and let it dry out or freeze it for later use. Molds, deckles, and other equipment should be hosed down and any remaining pulp picked off. Pay attention to felts and couching cloths, brushing off any remaining bits of pulp and washing cloths as needed. If you've used sizing or methyl-cellulose in your vat to strengthen casting pulp, be sure to wash your felts and cloths.

Embossed or Low-Relief Cast Paper

WET PULP or handmade paper that has been rewetted will pick up the textures and shapes of relatively flat objects pressed into it. Coins, wire, keys, string, textured fabrics, brass stencils, ceramic tiles, jewelry, etc., can all be used to create interesting dimensional designs in a sheet of paper. One method of capturing the image is to couch a relatively thick sheet of paper and then place the items you wish to emboss directly on top of the wet pulp, covering the sheet and embossing items with a couple of felts to cushion the items. Then press the sheet, letting everything remain in place until the sheet is dry.

Unveiling the dry embossing is always exciting, but sometimes surprising, too. I once embossed a pair of manicure scissors, thinking it would be interesting to show scissors captured by paper instead of the other way around. What I didn't consider, however, was that the scissors would rust from resting in the wet pulp. The result was a very mottled brown embossing of scissors in an otherwise white sheet. Fabrics and lace will also sometimes impart color when they are pressed into a wet sheet, actually adding to the design.

As you will find, your choice of approaches to producing original embossed or low-relief cast paper is as broad as the number of things that inspire you to create art. Exploring different ways to achieve embossing for wall sculpture, dimensional book or box covers, or even handmade cards can lead you down some fascinating paths with technical and personal discoveries along the way.

EMBOSSING A REDAMPENED SHEET OF PAPER

Many papermakers, like Marjorie Tomchuk, prefer to make their handmade paper, let it completely dry, and then rewet it when it is time to create embossed or sculptural paper art. Marjorie's embossed works are often large, and although they are quite strong, contain no internal sizing. Marjorie believes she gets a better and deeper embossing

CROSSINGS, EMBOSSED AND AIRBRUSHED HANDMADE PAPER WITH COLLAGED PHOTOS BY MARJORIE TOMCHUK

without it. The night before Marjorie plans to emboss a sheet, she uses a large sponge to rewet one side of a 36 x 25-inch sheet of her thick handmade cotton-fiber paper to begin softening it. She lets the wetted paper rest overnight so that the water is thoroughly and evenly distributed throughout the sheet when she is ready to work with it.

To create her art, Marjorie first constructs her embossing plate, which is assembled very much like a collage, on a matboard base that has been sealed with gesso or an acrylic medium. Marjorie adds dimensional pieces that are about the same thickness. When she uses an etching press to emboss her paper, the pieces must be limited to between 1/8-inch and 1/4-inch in height. Some of the materials she might choose to construct the plate include rubber sheeting, double-thickness matboard, Premo polymer clay, stones like those found in fish tanks, bamboo skewers, Saftey-Kut printmaking blocks, acrylic modeling paste, and other miscellaneous items such as washers, buttons, etc. Articles are chosen, of course, because the textures and shapes they impart relate to Marjorie's theme for each work, whether it be a work suggestive of nature or an architectural structure.

After Marjorie designs, assembles, and glues all of the elements of her embossing plate in place on the matboard base, she coats everything with white acrylic gesso to make it waterproof. When her "master plate" is dry, it is ready to receive the dampened sheet of handmade paper. Although Marjorie could emboss the soft wet sheet by pressing it by hand into the embossing plate with a sponge, it is easier and faster to use the etching press. After the embossed paper is completely dry, Marjorie uses an airbrush to apply fabric dyes. She also masks out some areas in preparation for adding color directly with a paintbrush. Marjorie finishes some of her embossings by collaging a digital photo to them.

Marjorie's inspiration for her work comes from many places. She notes that the content of her work has always had a direct tie to

Crossings, along with its embossing plate on the etching press.

LEFT Marjorie applying fabric dyes to the embossed work *Water and Ice* with an airbrush.
BELOW Marjorie's finished work *Water and Ice* after airbrushing.

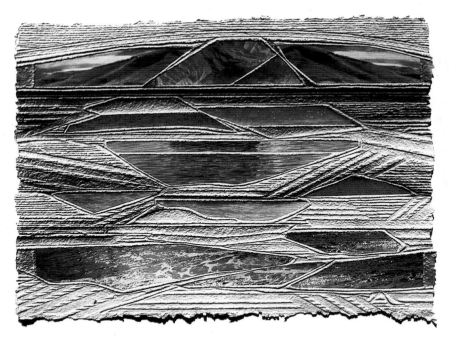

her environment. "Having traveled worldwide, my art depicts scenes from everywhere. At times these are highly abstract since my original experience will serve as a point of departure for the final image. Most often inspiration comes from a 'common' landscape. The qualities of abstract design, color, and balance are all integrated and play an important role in the final creation."

EMBOSSING WITH WET PULP

Leslie Ebert also creates deeply embossed handmade paper, but she prefers to work with wet pulp and casts her paper on top of the plate or block that will impart texture to her sheet. She sometimes couches on top of tapestry fabrics that have a distinct high- and low-textured surface, but notes that laying a sheet of wet pulp over bunched up paper bags or wrinkled felt will also produce interesting abstract designs. Most of the time, Leslie creates her sculptural paper by couching on top of a block that she has carved.

Leslie begins a design by creating a pencil drawing, keeping in mind that the shape of the block she will eventually carve and its linear border can also become part of the composition. As she draws her design, Leslie plans out the carving directions, making sure that her design is well composed—that it has "a focal point, movement, and a place for the eye to rest." After the pencil drawing is done, Leslie transfers it to her block by rubbing the back of the paper with a bone folder. Then she follows her pencil drawing,

carving out white areas of the design. Leslie works with a carving material called Safety-Kut. She prefers it to linoleum block since its thickness allows her to cut deeper into it. Made of rubber, Safety-Kut is also quite easy to carve with wood- or linoleum-carving tools and is available in large sheets, which also allows Leslie to make plates for her very large castings.

Like Marjorie Tomchuk, Leslie prefers to work with white undyed pulp and color it later. She makes a blend of pulp by boiling scraps of short-fibered cotton rag matboard and adding them to a vat of longer fibers, such as abaca, hemp, or sisal. This mixture gives Leslie a silky pulp that will produce the necessary thick sheet. At the end of the blending or beating process, Leslie also adds an internal sizing to strengthen her paper and calcium carbonate "to neutralize any acids that the artwork might be exposed to in the future." (Papermaking supply catalogs and websites usually offer a list of possible additives and their uses to help you decide what might be appropriate for your individual project.)

Leslie carving a large sheet of Safety-Kut to create a new work.

Draining excess water from the mold in preparation for couching.

Hand-forming the edges of the newly couched sheet.

Leslie's paints and a number of small works ready for airbrushing.

Adding a second color to a series of embossed works from the *Harlequin* suite.

A completed airbrushed work from the *Harlequin* suite.

ELDERS, A CAST PAPER WORK BY LESLIE EBERT

When her pulp is sufficiently beaten, Leslie dips her mold and deckle into the floating pulp at a slight angle, scooping up the pulp, and then shifts them to a horizontal position before shaking them to mesh the paper fibers. She then removes the deckle, drains excess water from the mold, and sponges the back of the sheet to remove additional water. Next she couches the sheet and continues to sponge off excess water as she presses the pulp into the depressions in her carved plate.

When the sheet is dry, she brushes it with an external sizing. After the sizing has dried, Leslie airbrushes the sheet with inks, dyes, watercolors, and acrylic pigments, working from light to dark to "float the paint over the surface," giving her colors the appearance of a soft, blended wash. She often goes back in to emphasize details by adding marks with oil sticks or pastels. Finally, each work is given several thin coats of clear acrylic spray to protect it and increase its longevity.

Scottish papermaker and bookbinder Joanne Kaar makes engaging embossed covers for her handmade books by carving linoleum block. She draws a simple design directly on the block and then irons the linoleum to heat it, rendering it softer and easier to cut. She casts directly onto the linoleum and covers it with a couching cloth before sponging firmly to make sure the paper is forced into the carved depressions in the linoleum. Many of Joanne's images are based on her surroundings. In her fascinating book *Papermaking and Bookbinding: Coastal Inspirations*, she explains, "I live on the far North coast of Scotland, and the sea and all it casts ashore are an ever-changing source of inspiration." Joanne's embossings show images and textures reminiscent of shells, fish, weathered wood, and brightly painted fishing boats.

On Pigments

Many papermakers, including Joanne Kaar, prefer to dye a quantity of partially processed plant materials—like cotton linters—called "half stuff," squeeze out the excess water, and let the colored pulp dry. The balls of pulp can be soaked in water at a later date and then processed in a blender to make sheets of paper. Joanne notes that you can "mix different colors of dyed pulp together like paints to make a more personal range of colored papers."

Dyed paper pulp that has been formed into balls and dried.

Joanne Kaar carving linoleum block to create a plate for an embossed book cover.

Joanne's handmade paper books with embossed shell design covers. Photo by Michael O'Donnell.

Dimensional Cast Paper

LIGHTWEIGHT and dramatic relief sculpture can be created by casting wet sheets of pulp or strained wet pulp over dimensional objects or into a mold made from any nonporous material. You can cast over existing objects like glass bowls, plastic containers, and shells or into cookie molds, muffin tins, or commercial papermaking molds found in craft stores. Open objects like cookie cutters will yield a variety of shaped designs. Loose pulp can also be cast into a mold created from Hydrocal plaster to produce fully three-dimensional works like Barbara Fletcher's *Chameleon* below.

CHAMELEON, A MOLD-CAST WORK BY BARBARA FLETCHER
Barbara presses several layers of loose pulp into her molds to give her works extra strength. Photo by Jan Bindes.

CASTING OVER OBJECTS

Leslie Ebert often casts over pieces of plaster or carved wood to produce works with faithful architectural detail like the one pictured below left. She also sometimes uses plasticine modeling clay to create a built-up mold rather than a carved one. She cautions that wood and clay forms need to be coated with a release agent such as Pam or silicone spray to prevent the paper from bonding with the mold. Styrofoam blocks can also be used to build up a mold. They are easy to carve or glue together to form various shapes. Because it is so lightweight, the Styrofoam can be left inside the cast paper to give it added strength and structure. Various sizes and shapes of lightweight armatures can become a hidden part of a cast paper structure.

Jeanne Petrosky often shapes her stone-colored papers around an angular foam base to create rocklike structures or square and rectangular bases to create groups of lustrous tiles.

The series of images opposite shows Jeanne at work, creating a piece for a large commissioned work. She explains that first she carves the foam armature that will give the structural shape to her handmade paper sculpture. She then sets up various vats of pigmented cotton pulp that she has blended from primary colors to create a range of earth tones.

She uses a mold and deckle to gather her pulp and, instead of couching on a couching cloth, transfers the newly formed sheet to a piece of acrylic where she can

For this work, Leslie Ebert cast her paper over plaster molding to capture the molding's architectural detail.

By shaping her paper pulp around foam armatures Jeanne Petrosky creates structures suggestive of rock formations.

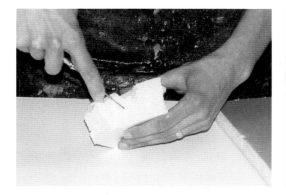

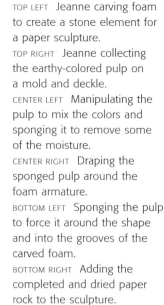

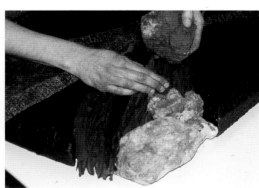

TOP LEFT Jeanne carving foam to create a stone element for a paper sculpture.

TOP RIGHT Jeanne collecting the earthy-colored pulp on a mold and deckle.

CENTER LEFT Manipulating the pulp to mix the colors and sponging it to remove some of the moisture.

CENTER RIGHT Draping the sponged pulp around the foam armature.

BOTTOM LEFT Sponging the pulp to force it around the shape and into the grooves of the carved foam.

BOTTOM RIGHT Adding the completed and dried paper rock to the sculpture.

continue to manipulate the fluid pulp to further mix colors. Next, she sponges the sheet to remove some of the moisture. While the sheet is still damp, she applies it over the carved armature and continues sponging into the realistic grooves and indentations she has created, removing still more moisture. The cotton paper shrinks around the armature as it dries, conforming to the shape Jeanne has carved. When all elements of the work are in place, Jeanne coats the work with methylcellulose archival glue to seal it. She applies luster pigments on top of the stones or tiles to give them a natural-looking glow.

Of her creative process Jeanne says, "Something occurs that enables me to create a mood—sensual, calm, playful, secure, or organic with line, texture, and balance—using handmade paper. I do become inspired by simplicity, including that of Japanese culture. Elements of nature intrigue me along with the interaction of people and all our different, yet similar natures. The humbling, yet exciting, part is that I often don't have a clue where to begin, so I just start, listen, and observe what is happening. I can't, nor do I want to, plan the whole piece. Being creative in anything is more of a matter of showing up and letting things evolve as they wish."

SHEET CASTING

Whole sheets or torn strips of couched paper can be cast into or placed over objects to create three-dimensional paper art. To create a dimensional structure using sheet casting, first sponge your couched paper to remove most of the moisture. It can be transported on its couching sheet and draped over bowls, rods, plasticine sculptures, or whatever mold you have chosen or created. Couched sheets can also be eased into concave structures or molds.

To build up a strong laminated structure, tear off strips of the couched sheet and place them in position on your casting form. Overlap the feathered edges of the torn sheets as you press them in place with a sponge or tamp them into place with a small stiff-bristled brush. The feathered edge will help create a strong bond and help hide seams in your finished work.

CASTING WITH LOOSE PULP

Loose pulp can be used to build up an exceptionally strong three-dimensional structure by casting it into a found mold, such as a bowl, or into a plaster mold as Barbara Fletcher does (opposite). To create a thick casting material to fill a mold, lift some pulp from your vat and strain it to remove some of the water. Apply the pulp with your hands and press it evenly into your mold, letting some of it extend, if you wish, to create a deckle edge. Use a damp sponge to apply pressure to compact the pulp and wick off some of the moisture. Wring the sponge out as you work. Removing more moisture will lessen drying time, which can take several days.

Some papermakers like to add methylcellulose to their pulp to give the casting more bonding strength. Since methylcellulose is glue, however, adding it can

CEREMONIAL BOWL #2, A DIMENSIONAL CAST-PAPER WORK BY BETSY R. MIRAGLIA
Acrylic stenciling, wood, wire, and monoprinted glassine were used in the work.

sometimes make removing cast paper from detailed molds more difficult, so be sure to use a release agent when working with it.

When the cast paper is dry, peel it from the mold. Use a dull knife, if necessary, to help ease it out. If you have difficulty getting your mold to release, next time try coating it with Pam and then rinsing it with warm water before applying the pulp. Butcher's wax or a commercial release agent available from a supplier can also be used. Try casting with pulps that have been dyed different colors to create variegated works.

You can work with colored pulp, or paint the cast paper after it is dry. Barbara Fletcher's amazing whimsical cast paper sculptures are made by pressing loose pulp into plaster molds in several layers to give them added strength. She usually begins her casting process by sculpting a form in non-hardening plasticine clay or foam, which can take a few hours or up to 20 hours for a large, highly dimensional sculpture.

TIP

Be sure that any form you create in plasticine clay doesn't contain undercut areas, because they will transfer to the mold you create from the clay. If paper pulp is then pressed into the recessed areas of your mold, it will wind up permanently attached to it!

For an uncomplicated form like the frog body (page 25), Barbara sometimes recycles small pieces of foam and molds them into a form with the assistance of duct tape. (Another use for the miracle tape!) The next step is to decide whether the form needs to be cast in several sections. If the form, such as the frog sculpture, needs to be divided, a sharp knife is used to create a deep line and divide the form into sections. Strips of plastic are put in the dividing lines to keep the sections separate. (The legs or other appendages of Barbara's creatures are often cast in separate molds and added to the main paper sculpture when the other sections are all adhered together.)

Barbara Fletcher's frog form created with foam, duct tape, and clay, divided into two parts with strips of plastic, ready to be covered with hydrocal plaster.

Covering the frog form with plaster.

Then the sculpture is covered with hydrocal plaster. The plaster takes about 45 minutes to set and 24 hours for it to dry and cure. When the plaster is finally dry, the mold is separated and the clay, foam, or duct-taped sculptural form around which the mold was made is removed.

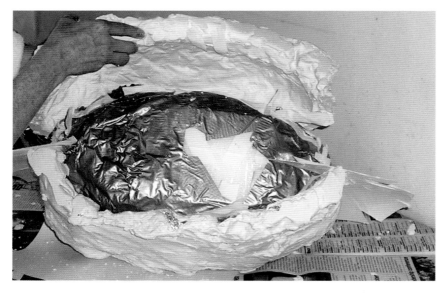

Then Barbara can place wet pulp on a screen to drain off some of the water and begin handpressing it into the plaster mold. Barbara uses recycled papers and brightly colored construction paper to make her pulp. The papers already have binding agents in them, so she only needs to add retention aid to keep colors from fading.

Because a large work can take a week to air dry, Barbara has built a special oven to speed up the drying time. The oven consists of a large tin box with insulation and light bulbs, and air holes for circulation. She notes that no mold release is required, because the paper shrinks as it dries and can be removed from the plaster cast quite easily. When Barbara uses colored pulps to make castings she also airbrushes the dry sculpture with Procion fabric dyes, using stencil and resist techniques to intensify the colors and luminosity of her pieces. The sculptures are then coated with a protective acrylic spray.

Barbara began making her fantasy creatures in handmade paper after taking a fantasy illustration course many years ago. The work of Dutch painter Hieronymus Bosch has also influenced her art. She has made many animal, insect, fish, and bird sculptures for notable collectors, including writer Stephen King, for whom she made many fantasy creatures that hung suspended over an indoor pool.

TOP Separating the mold that now bears the frog shape.
ABOVE Pressing the wet pulp into the mold.
RIGHT Removing the plaster mold from the dried cast paper.

Manipulating Paper for Sculptural Effects

DRY SHEETS of soft handmade paper can be molded around a form and manipulated to create sculptural works. Calligrapher Sharon Hanse tore the edges of several different colored sheets of dry handmade paper and then rolled them around a paper towel holder to curl them; then they were nested inside each other and affixed with Yes! paste to form her beautiful cocoonlike structure *Sacred*. *Rock* was created from dry and slightly rewetted handmade paper that was elevated with pieces of foamcore to give it dimension; each layer of handmade paper has a circular torn center, which Sharon made by using a stylus to incise a circle and then dropping water into the circular

groove to rewet the circle enough to facilitate its removal from the rest of the sheet.

Individual sheets of dried and then rewetted handmade paper can also be manipulated into rocklike sculptural forms, as witnessed in the stunning work of Jeanne Petrosky, whose sheets of handmade paper are often gathered and layered in free-flowing abstract forms. Jeanne explains that she "creates dimensional environments by contrasting full sheets with multiple layering, focusing on the jagged or 'deckle' edge intrinsic to the papermaking process. The work blends texture, color, and balance in such a way that invites the imagination to question,

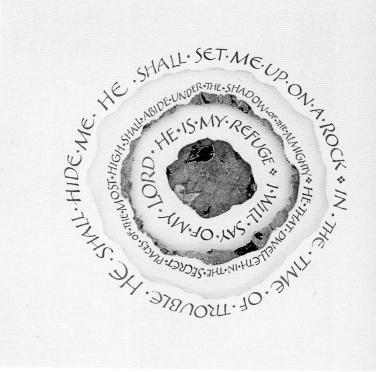

ABOVE *ROCK*, HANDMADE PAPER COLLAGE AND CALLIGRAPHY BY SHARON LEE HANSE
LEFT *SACRED*, PAPER SCULPTURE AND CALLIGRAPHY BY SHARON LEE HANSE

explore, and enjoy." Like Marjorie Tomchuk, Jeanne uses 100 percent cotton linters for their strength, but prefers to dye her pulp in the vat rather than after her work is formed. She begins by couching onto a Plexiglas sheet and further mixing pulps in their very wet state. Then she sponges the paper to absorb as much water as she can, and lets it completely dry. She rewets the sheet by spraying it until it is damp enough to become pliable. Then Jeanne hand-forms it into the desired shape and inserts the new handmade paper strip into the sculpture.

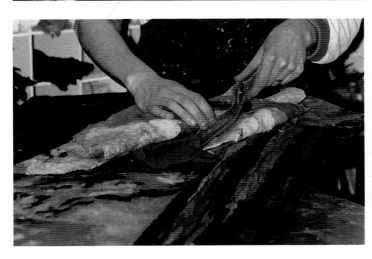

FAR LEFT, TOP TO BOTTOM Jeanne Petrosky rewetting the paper to make it pliable, rolling the dampened paper into the desired shape, and inserting the dry reformed paper into the paper sculpture.

LEFT One of Jeanne's free-flowing abstract works, created entirely of handmade paper. It was constructed using the same methods illustrated at left.

In addition to casting paper into carved linoleum block to produce dimensional covers for her handmade books, Joanne Kaar creates sculptural covers by couching on top of string. The work she produces this way is suggestive of deep crevices in coastal rocks. She sandwiches string between two wet sheets of contrasting colored paper as she couches one sheet on top of another, as shown below, and then pulls the string to artfully tear the sheets apart. Then she uses her fingers to accentuate the gash and manipulate the sheets to make the division between the sheets deeper, wider, and more irregular. She allows the sheets to dry in place to keep the torn paper as sculptural as possible.

RIGHT Couching the paper on top of the string.
FAR RIGHT Pulling the string to form the sculptural tear.
BELOW Joanne B. Kaar's sculptural books, suggestive of crevices in coastal rocks. Photos by Michael O'Donnell.

Pulp Painting

If COLORED PULP is watered down so that it is quite runny, and then placed in a squeeze bottle or turkey baster, you can draw and paint with it. Many artists work with a palette of dyed pulps kept in plastic bags or containers that they can store in the refrigerator between paintings. Formation aid, a substance that helps to disperse and suspend the pulp's fibers, and make it easier for them to interlock, can be added to help keep the pulp from clogging the applicator.

There are various ways to create a pulp painting. Anne Kenyon sometimes begins a piece by pouring wet pulp on a mold and deckle; an action she describes as being "much like pouring wet paint." The colors that she pours together can form a finished sheet that resembles a sky with clouds, foliage, or reflections in water. She notes that you can also pour pulp into a shaped deckle placed over another layer of pulp.

Other techniques involve squirting or spooning wet pulp on the mold and then couching onto a newly formed wet sheet of paper, or squirting pulp directly on a newly couched sheet. Hands, too, can be used to place strained pulp in position on a wet sheet of paper that will serve as a canvas and bond with the pulp when pressed and dried. Although many pulp paintings tend to be more textural than dimensional, some, especially those in which the artist places the strained pulp in position by hand, tend to have quite a bit of relief.

EGRET WADING (11 × 13 INCHES), A PULP PAINTING BY ANNE KENYON The reeds in the background of this piece were created by adding cut slivers of paper to the wet pulp on the mold and pouring a thin layer of pulp over them to hold them in place. The water was pulp-poured as one piece of paper and then a similar piece was torn and pasted with matte medium to enhance the ripples in the water.

OCTOBER COWS, A PULP PAINTING BY ANNE KENYON The cows were built up in layers and the blue-black paper for their spots was couched on Mylar to give them a very smooth surface.

Betsy Miraglia's unique method of pulp painting involves working on Plexiglas, but in a radically different way than Jeanne Petrosky. Betsy makes her own pulp using abaca fibers. After beating the fibers, she colors the pulp with Aardvark liquid colored pigments. A color-coded drawing is placed on the underside of a piece of Plexiglas, and partially strained colored pulps are laid onto the Plexiglas, where they are eventually sponged lightly and left to dry. When the paper work is completely dry, it easily releases from the Plexiglas. At this point she can print, stencil, paint, etc., onto the dry surface of the piece. About her working method, Betsy says, "The three-dimensional process allows me to build up different levels of color, as well as texture and space. The shapes of the flat areas are determined by the overall design of the larger finished image. I don't always work in a rectangular or square shape, so the Plexiglas technique allows me to form many abstract shapes."

When totally dry, the shapes are removed from the Plexiglas and layered to create a complex image. The individual pieces are separated by archival corrugated board, which allows the air to flow through the layers and helps prevent a lifting of the separating boards. The boards are glued to the backs of the shapes with clear window caulking. She glues the lowest level, backed with a piece of corrugated board slightly smaller than the shape, onto her linen-wrapped mounting board. The next layer, also backed with corrugated board, is then glued into position, and so on. She weights each section for at least 4 hours to allow a tight bond before going to the next layer. *Transitional Change*, shown below, is an example of Betsy's beautiful multilevel inlaid pulp painting.

Betsy describes her work and her inspiration: "My handmade paper work is about ritual, the oneness of creating. It's about color, interaction, and space. It's about patience, time, and getting in touch with my inner spirit. It's about memories, a fear of forgetting, and about continually discovering new ways to record those memories through visual expression."

TRANSITIONAL CHANGE, A MULTILEVELED, STENCILED INLAID PULP PAINTING BY BETSY R. MIRAGLIA

UNTITLED (32 × 20 INCHES), CAST PAPER FORMS BY JEANNE PETROSKY
The dimensional environments Jeanne creates with her paper sculpture reflect her interest in the natural world and in the simplicity of the Japanese culture. The rigid rock-inspired structures in this work are perfectly balanced by the flowing deckle edges of the handmade paper she has inserted between them. To give her art a natural-looking glow, Jeanne coats each sculptural element with archival glue and applies luster pigments.

STONE GARLAND (10 × 29 INCHES), CAST PAPER BY LESLIE EBERT
Like most of Leslie's cast paper works, *Stone Garland* was created from undyed pulp. After the piece dried, Leslie applied a soft blended wash with an airbrush and emphasized details with oil pastels.

OLD TOWN (25 × 36 INCHES), AN EMBOSSING BY MARJORIE TOMCHUK
This embossed cityscape, like many of Marjorie's works, was inspired by her worldwide travels. It was done on artist-made paper using the artist's own digital photography collaged into the paper.

PEACE (16 × 20 INCHES), A MIXED-MEDIA WORK BY BETSY R. MIRAGLIA
This work, comprised of handmade paper, elements of handmade books, and mixed media, was inspired by Indian spirit bags that were used to carry medicines and personal possessions. The fringe areas are cut pieces of handmade paper, wrinkled and beaded. The tin horns symbolize noisemakers used to chase evil spirits away.

CHAPTER 2

Mastering
FOLDED-PAPER DESIGNS

ORIGAMI, probably the best-known paper-folding technique, is the basis for many other folded designs. Some of these designs are modifications of traditional origami structures that were created hundreds of years ago. This chapter will show you how to create two traditional origami designs, a bowl and a lily, and alter them slightly to give them a more modern look. You'll also learn to make some exciting book and card forms such as caterpillar books, diamond-fold maze books, star cards, and exploding cards that have their roots in origami.

After providing some basic information on working with paper that is to be incorporated into demensional projects, the chapter moves on to a very easy technique called accordion folding or pleating. Although not directly related to origami, accordion folding will give you practice scoring and folding your paper into the same mountains and valleys you'll use in origami. By following this elemental zigzag folding technique, you can create books or cards in a horizontal, vertical, or triangular format with all manner of variations, cut work, and attachments. Accordion folds can be enjoyed on their own or can be added to other structures so that they spill forward when the structure is opened, as seen in Fred Mullett's caterpillar book (page 47) or project from a work like Susan Share's papier-mâché mask (page 108). Accordion folding is a most versatile technique, a perfect starting point for learning how to master paper folding.

OPPOSITE *FACETED TOWER*, AN ORIGAMI WORK BY DEBRA GLANZ.

3-D Paper Techniques

EQUIPMENT

You'll need the following equipment to begin your adventures in three-dimensional paper arts. If you are new to paper arts, this section will teach you some basic techniques to insure that your projects turn out well. Practice cutting and gluing on scrap paper first.

BURNISHING TOOL A bone or Teflon folder can be used to sharpen paper folds and help bond glued papers.

GLUE BRUSHES Large and small glue brushes will be useful for many three-dimensional paper projects.

METAL-EDGED RULER OR TRIANGLE You'll need a metal-edged ruler to guide your scoring and handheld cutting tools. If possible, get a metal-edged transparent triangle. C-Thru rulers have a wonderful grid that makes measuring easy.

SCORING TOOL An awl, bone folder, or ball-tipped burnisher will make a good scoring tool.

VARIOUS CUTTING TOOLS You'll need a self-healing cutting mat, a mat knife, an X-Acto knife and blades, and scissors. A large paper cutter or rotary trimmer would also be helpful.

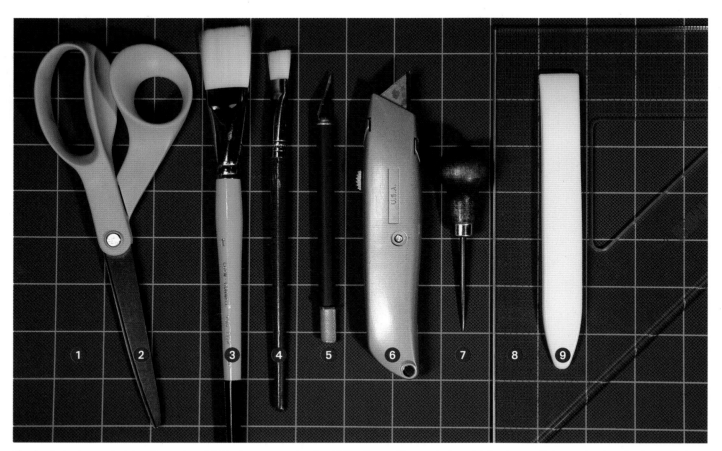

The basic tools needed for dimensional folded paper works: 1. self-healing cutting mat; 2. pair of scissors; 3. large glue brush; 4. small glue brush; 5. X-Acto knife with a #11 blade (for cutting papers); 6. mat knife (for cutting through heavy book- or matboard); 7. awl (for scoring papers); 8. metal-edged C-Thru plastic triangle; 9. Teflon folder.

BASIC 3-D PAPER TECHNIQUES

Although there is something very special about making a three-dimensional paper structure by starting from scratch with paper pulp, there are many creative ways to use purchased papers—whether handmade by others, mold-made, or machine-made—to build paper sculptures, boxes, origami, pop-up cards, lanterns, dimensional books, etc. Some of the structures, like the pop-up cards, must be made with heavy rigid paper. Others, like the origami lilies, need to be done with a thinner paper so that the lily's many folds can be made. Although some papers require that they be handled in a particular manner because of their specific properties, it is still a good idea to learn some basic techniques that will apply to working with the majority of the papers you'll use in dimensional paper projects. The following basic techniques will help you "tame" the paper you work with and assure that your dimensional paper projects are well constructed.

FINDING A PAPER'S GRAIN

The fibers of handmade and mold-made papers are distributed at random throughout a sheet and do not have a particular grain direction, which means they can be folded or shaped in any direction. Machine-made papers, matboards, and bookboard, however, have a distinct grain direction similar to the grain found in a plank of wood or a piece of fabric. It is important to determine and keep track of the grain direction of your papers and boards and make sure that they match when creating structures. Tearing and cutting papers will be much easier if you do so in a direction parallel to the grain of the paper. In general, papers will fold more easily, be less likely to crack when you attempt to crease them and will hold their shape better if you

make sure that your fold line runs parallel to the grain of the paper. When gluing papers and boards together it will also be very important that the grains of both materials match to prevent the materials from pulling against one aother and warping as they dry.

To test for grain direction in a sheet of paper, bend the sheet in half. If the paper easily collapses in on itself, you're bending with the grain. If the paper resists your efforts, you're bending cross grain. Test the paper in each direction and then pencil an arrow on it to mark the grain direction.

To test for grain direction in bookboard, hold the long edges of the whole sheet in your hands and attempt to bend it. Little resistance means the grain is running parallel to your arms. Considerable resistance means you're bending across the grain. Pencil an arrow on pieces of bookboard as you cut them so that you don't lose track of the grain direction—it's more difficult to test small pieces of heavy board.

Testing for grain direction in a sheet of paper.

SCORING

Scoring—using an awl or bone folder to crease a paper's surface—prepares a paper for folding. To score a sheet, hold a metal-edged ruler against the desired fold line and, using the ruler as a guide, drag the point of the tool down the length of the ruler.

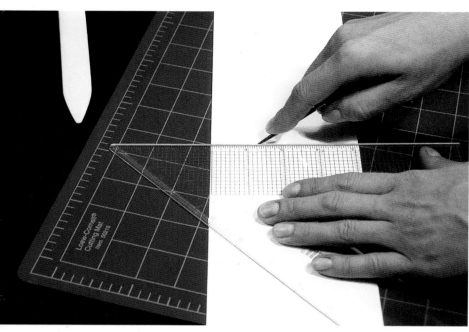

Scoring paper to prepare for folding it.

Burnishing a sheet of paper to help bond it to the board it covers.

You'll want to indent, not break, the surface of light- to medium-weight papers and bend away from, not into, the fold line. When working with very heavy papers you'll cut into the top layer of paper with an X-Acto knife to score it for folding.

BURNISHING

Burnishing paper with a bone or Teflon folder will sharpen a fold or help bond glued papers by pushing out wrinkles and air bubbles. To avoid damaging or adding a shine to papers being burnished, cover them with a sheet of tracing paper. When bonding one glued paper to another, hold the burnishing tool on its side and work from the center of the sheet outward to flatten it.

CUTTING PAPER AND BOARD

If you haven't invested in a good paper cutter, like a Kutrimmer, don't despair. It may take a bit longer, but you can easily divide paper and board by hand if you follow a few rules. Make sure you always have a sharp blade in your X-Acto or mat knife so that your cuts are clean instead of ragged. Hold the knife upright and slide it against the edge of a metal-edged rule to divide paper or board. Cut on a self-healing cutting mat; cutting on top of and into cardboard quickly dulls a knife blade. If you're trying to divide matboard or other heavy material, don't attempt to do so in one pass. Make several cuts instead, to neatly divide it.

TEARING PAPER

Most papers can also be divided by tearing them. You can create papers that have a pseudo deckle edge in a number of ways. An Art Deckle ruler can be used to tear even heavy watercolor papers and create an edge that almost looks like it was made with a papermaker's deckle. Simply hold the ruler in place over a sheet of paper, then tear the paper against the ruler's serrated edge.

Another way to divide paper or give it an interesting edge is to lay down a line of water with a pipette full of water or with a wet brush. Wait for the water to soak into the paper and then pull the paper apart. To create a free-form edge, let the brush wander; for a straight line, fold the paper or run the brush against the edge of the ruler. You can also use the method employed by Sharon Hanse when she created *Rock* (page 26). She used a stylus to create a circular indentation and then dripped water into it to facilitate removing a circular piece from a large sheet of paper. If you are tearing highly fibrous papers, it will be easier if you make sure that you are tearing with the grain.

Papers can also be torn without the help of water. Tear toward you to expose part of the paper's core (especially lovely with two-toned papers), or tear away from you to create a ragged and ruffled edge.

WORKING WITH ADHESIVES

Depending upon what type of dimensional art you are making and its intended life span, you may want to work with an archival glue or paste, a glue stick or a double-sided adhesive film like Cello-Mount, Stick-Ease, mounting tape, or the favorite of picture framers, Positional Mounting Adhesive (PMA). The benefit of working with a dry adhesive film is that you don't need to worry about paper buckling or the necessity of pressing the project under heavy books or boards to keep bookboards, wet with glue, from warping as they dry. The drawback is that if you are not working with a repositional adhesive, like PMA, and you place your paper or bookboard in the wrong spot, you are quite literally *stuck*. Recommendations for various types of adhesives will be made with individual projects.

Dividing paper with an X-Acto knife.

Accordion-Fold Designs

Many different types of papers—handmade, mold-made, or machine-made—can be used for folded designs, depending upon the thickness of the paper and whether you are trying to achieve a crisp- or soft-edged design.

SIMPLE ACCORDION-FOLD, or concertina, designs are great structures to use for creating three-dimensional paper art. An accordion-fold card can be just one long piece of folded paper that, if made from a sturdy stock, can stand by itself to display a message, show off ephemera glued to the front and back of its pages, or house pop-ups and fold-down surprises. If hard covers are added to the paper, the card can become an accordion-fold book, taking on a sculptural form when opened out and allowed to stand on its own. It can also become a tassel book or hanging ornament if the ends are adhered together. The accordion-fold structure can also be used as a support for a tunnel book, as a base for a pop-up flag book, or as a pattern for a standing screen.

GETTING STARTED

If you've never worked with paper to create a three-dimensional piece, I recommend that you first study the section called 3-D Paper Techniques at the beginning of this chapter (pages 36–39) before tackling the folded-paper designs in this chapter or the projects in the following three chapters.

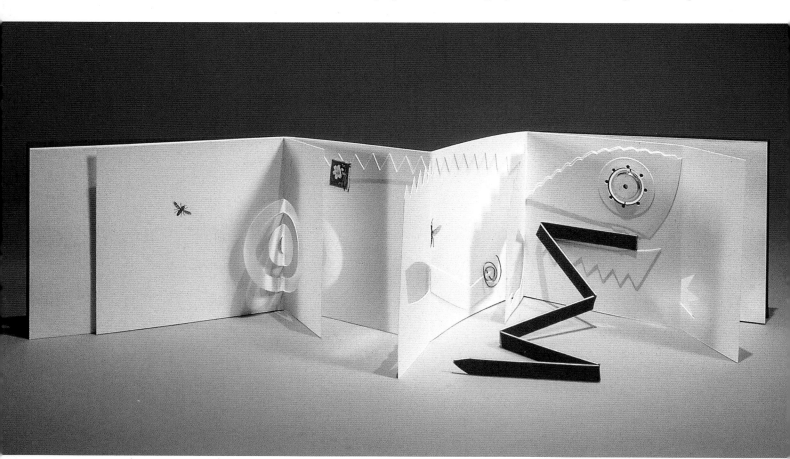

OUT TO LUNCH, AN ACCORDION-FOLD BOOK WITH FLAPS, FOLDOUTS, CUTOUTS, AND FOUND OBJECTS BY ANNE-CLAUDE COTTY

CREATING AN ACCORDION-FOLD CARD

You may already know how to make an accordion fold, creasing a single sheet of paper into a series of *mountains* (with the crease of the fold pointing up) and *valleys* (with the crease of the fold pointing down). If you need a refresher course, here are the directions for making an accordion-fold card—a great jumping-off point for other structures.

1 Cutting the pages

Use a paper cutter or a mat knife and a ruler to cut a long strip of cover-weight paper for the pages of your accordion-fold structure. The grain should run vertical, parallel to the vertical fold lines, and the width of the strip should match the measurement you choose for the height of the pages. Don't worry about the length; you can cut several strips and join them later to make a structure as long as you wish.

2 Folding the pages

Prepare to fold the pages by measuring off each page width for the entire length of the paper strip and making a faint mark with the tip of your awl or a needle. Place your squaring triangle at every other mark and score the paper by lightly running an awl or weaving needle against the edge of the triangle. Then turn the paper over and score the remaining pages on the opposite side of the paper. Use your bone folder to crease the paper (away from the indentation) to create the first accordion-fold page. Keep accordion-folding until you reach the end of your paper, making sure that the top and bottom edges of the paper always line up. To lengthen the structure, join similarly folded pages together, as shown. Finish your strip by cutting off any excess that's not wide enough to be used as a page or that folds in the wrong direction for your design.

On Folding

A renegade method of folding, which goes much faster, can be accomplished by measuring and scoring for the first fold and then turning the paper over and using the first folded page as a guide to determine where to score and fold the next. If you keep turning your paper over, make sure the tops and bottoms of your pages line up and always use the *previous* fold as a guide. You may find, as I do, that this method works perfectly and that page size remains constant without expanding throughout your folding. Although this method is frowned upon by many and deemed impossible by some, it's worth a try. You may find it works just fine.

WHAT YOU'LL NEED

Awl

Bone folder

Cover-weight paper

Mat knife

Long metal-edged ruler or triangle

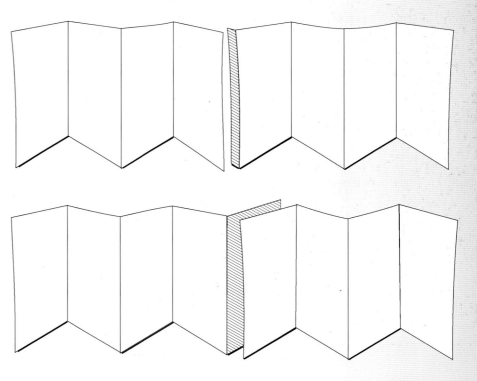

To create a longer set of accordion-fold pages, overlap and glue folded strips together using either method shown here.

CREATING AN ACCORDION-FOLD BOOK

WHAT YOU'LL NEED

Bone folder

Bookboard to create the hard covers

Cover-weight paper for the interior pages

Light- to medium-weight decorative paper

Mat knife

Metal-edged ruler or triangle

PVA (polyvinyl acetate) glue and glue brush

Ribbon or cord to tie the book closed (optional)

Scrap paper

Tracing paper

By placing your accordion-fold pages within hard covers, you can quickly create a more durable card or an accordion-fold book. Some accordion-fold books are composed of several strips of paper spliced together and measure many feet in length, meandering across a room when on display. When making a book, you'll want to make the covers first and then measure and fold pages to fit within the covers.

1 Cutting the cover boards

Decide what size you'd like your book to be and then transfer the measurements to a piece of bookboard. Make sure that the grain of your board runs vertically (see page 37 for instructions on how to determine the grain of machine-made paper). Use a mat knife and a ruler or a professional paper cutter to cut out front and back cover boards. Check to be sure that the corners are cut at right angles and that edges are straight. If the cutting has left ragged edges on your board, lightly sand them. Lightly pencil a line noting the grain direction on your cover boards.

2 Preparing the cover papers

Determine grain direction on the paper you've chosen to cover the bookboards. Arrange it on your worktable so that the grain matches your bookboard and then cut two pieces, each 1 inch wider and longer than the book covers. This will allow for a $1/2$-inch border of paper to overlap each cover board.

3 Gluing the boards in place

Prepare to glue up the front cover by placing it on a sheet of scrap paper. Working from the center outward, brush a thin layer of glue onto it. Then place it glue-side-down in the center of the wrong side of your decorative sheet. Immediately discard the scrap paper and wipe any glue from your hands before turning the decorative paper and attached bookboard right-side-up. Place a piece of tracing paper or scrap paper over the decorative paper and, using a bone folder, work from the center of the board outward to burnish out any air bubbles or wrinkles.

Paul Maurer's lively lettering is featured on the inside of this accordion-fold book by Diane Maurer-Mathison.

TOP LEFT Trimming the corners off the cover papers to begin mitering the corners of the accordion-fold book covers.

TOP RIGHT Brushing glue on one of the long edges of paper.

BOTTOM LEFT Standing the book on end in preparation for rolling it down. After the glued edge is in place, you can use your thumb or a bone folder to apply pressure and adhere it.

BOTTOM RIGHT Burnishing the glued edge to press out any wrinkles.

4 Gluing down the first flaps of the cover paper

After burnishing, turn the paper and board-over again onto a clean piece of scrap paper so that the bookboard is again facing up. Miter the corners by cutting off the corners of the decorative paper, leaving about $1/8$- to $1/4$-inch between the edge of the board and the end of the paper. Generally, twice the thickness of the bookboard is a sufficient margin of paper to leave to cover the board corners. Apply glue to one of the longer edges of paper, running the brush against the edge of the bookboard as you work, and fold the flap of paper over the bookboard to glue it down. (I like to stand the book on it's edge for a moment and then lower it until it is flat, to press the flap of paper down.) Use your thumb and then the bone folder to smooth the edge of the cover paper against the side of the bookboard. Burnish the paper down so that it has no wrinkles or loose edges. Now glue down the other longer edge of decorative paper and burnish it until it's smooth.

5 Finishing the mitered corners

Create well-mitered corners by using your index fingernail or the tip of the bone folder to tuck in the small overlap of paper (indicated by the arrow in the diagram at right) that appears when the long edges of the paper are folded over. This overlap, the result of leaving the $1/4$-inch space between the paper and the board, will prevent the corners of the board from showing when the short flaps of decorative paper are folded over. Once the overlaps are tucked in place (angled slightly toward each other), apply glue to the remaining short flaps, then fold over and burnish in place.

On Mitering

Mitering refers to the way that papers are cut or folded, fitted together at the corners of the boards they cover, and glued in place. It is wise to practice this operation a few times, since a poor mitering job can ruin a project.

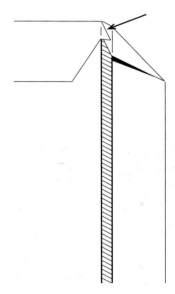

To create a tightly mitered corner, tuck in the little flap of paper indicated by the arrow.

Gluing the accordion-folded pages to the front book cover.

A tassel book by Lynne Carnes.

6 Assembling the accordion-fold book

Brush glue on the ends (endpapers) of your folded stack of pages (these should be about $1/4$-inch shorter and more narrow overall than your cover boards) and position them within hard covers so that an $1/8$-inch margin surrounds them. A larger margin can be left if you desire, but the page and board height should be very close if you wish your accordion-fold book to stand open for display. Use your bone folder over a sheet of tracing paper to burnish the endpapers down. Insert a sheet of waxed paper between the covers and the first and last pages of the book to keep any excess glue from penetrating and press the book under weights until dry.

ANOTHER IDEA

If the ends of a series of accordion-folded pages are adhered together, instead of being glued to book board, you can create a tassel book or hanging ornament, like the one by Lynne Carnes at left. Simply knot some narrow ribbon, embroidery floss, waxed linen cord, or similar material together, making sure you have enough strands to span each folded page. (Lynne has doubled her strands to form a loop at the top.) Place the strands in the recessed valley folds and knot them together to gather the folds of the structure. Beads and decorative knots can be added to further decorate the piece.

Tunnel Books

A TUNNEL BOOK is made up of a series of pages glued to accordion-folded, or concertina, sides that support them. The pages have openings or peepholes that decrease in size and allow you to see through one page to the next, for a telescopic view of the final uncut back page. A rigid support of bookboard or matboard is usually placed on the front and the back of the book to help it stand. There are many variations on the tunnel book format with modifications made to the pages or the accordion spines to keep the pages from projecting out at an angle as they would if simply glued to the concertina sides. One method I like, suggested by book artist Ed Hutchins, is to make a series of small M-shaped accordion-folded structures to hold the book together. By using these, and gluing to the flat planes of the sides of the M, instead of trying to adhere pages to a continuous accordion, angled pages can be prevented.

The tunnel book pictured here measures 5 × 7 inches and contains five pages held together with four sets of M-shaped supports on each side of the book. The supports are narrow enough to remain out of view when the book is seen from the front, and long enough to securely support the interior pages. To give the opening a more panoramic canyon view, I modified the tunnel format and allowed the opening in each page to decrease in height with only a slight change in width. The first and last pages are adhered to pieces of matboard. I also collaged additional papers onto the back of some of the paste paper pages. It's fun to explore the tunnel format using post-cards, photos, or drawings or creating more of a collage design as I have. The openings can be various sizes and shapes, as can the book itself.

Parts for the tunnel book.

The accordion spines join the tunnel book pages together.

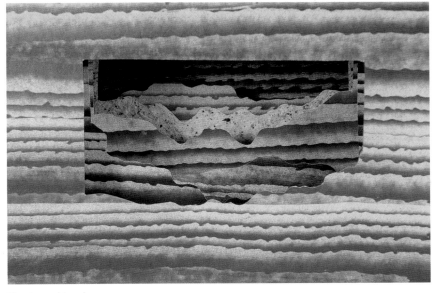

The tunnel book.

Diamond-Fold Designs

BY MAKING JUST THREE simple folds in a paper square you can create the versatile diamond fold, a nifty little structure on its own or combined in multiples.

To make a diamond fold, begin with a square paper and make a horizontal valley fold followed by a vertical valley fold. Then open the paper, flip it over and make a diagonal valley fold. Flip the paper again and push in the center, bringing two points together to create its dimensional shape.

Multiples of a diamond fold can be joined to create a structure called a star card ornament. The same structures, if attached differently, can be assembled to create an origami caterpillar book.

STAR CARD ORNAMENT

Lay out five individual pieces (each facing up), align their points, and use a dry adhesive to glue them together. There are two ways to hang the ornament. Holes can be punched in the first and last points and ribbon can be strung through the holes, or ribbon can be sandwiched between the first and last points and hard covers made for the card. Variations on the technique, such as those shown in the charming leaf-printed card by Lynne Carnes (opposite, top right), can be made by cutting the folded elements into interesting shapes before assembling them.

ORIGAMI CATERPILLAR BOOK

Elements for the caterpillar book are created in the same way as for the ornament, but the book is assembled by aligning the elements so that the point of one structure is slipped into the center of another. The two surfaces are then adhered together to create the book.

The diamond fold starts with a square of paper. Make two horizontal valley folds—one in each direction (A). Open the paper up, flip it over, and make a diagonal valley fold (B). Open the paper again, flip it again, and push in the center to collapse and finish the structure (C and D).

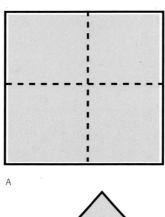

A

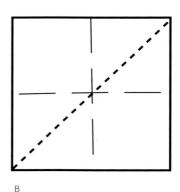

B

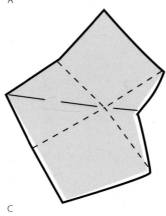

C

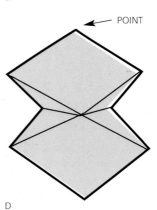

POINT

D

ABOVE Adhering the folded elements, points up, to create a star card ornament
RIGHT Lynne Carnes created this leaf-printed structure by cutting the edges of the folded elements to mimic the leaf outline before assembly.

To create a caterpillar book, adhere the folded elements with one point up and one down. The book and elements (with added tiny maze card, see next page) are by Fred B. Mullett.

DIAMOND-FOLD MAZE BOOK

Artist Mary Howe sent me a diagram for a maze book (also known as an *origami book*) that contains a diamond fold similar to the element used in the caterpillar book. The diamond folds in this book, however, are not created individually and then glued together; they remain attached to one another from the start. The book is created by folding a single sheet of paper and then cutting parts of the folds to open the sheet up. The sample shown was made from a piece of paper that measured $8\frac{1}{2} \times 17$ inches. Follow the diagram to form the appropriate mountain and valley folds. (Mary notes that it doesn't matter which you do first as long as you pay attention to which type of fold you are doing.) Cut the slits that open the paper after the folding is done, and then manipulate the diamond-shaped areas to form the a-maze-ing book.

Follow the diagram and make the mountain and valley folds before cutting the slits and manipulating the diamond folds to create the book.

———————	CUT
– – – – –	MOUNTAIN FOLD
··········	VALLEY FOLD

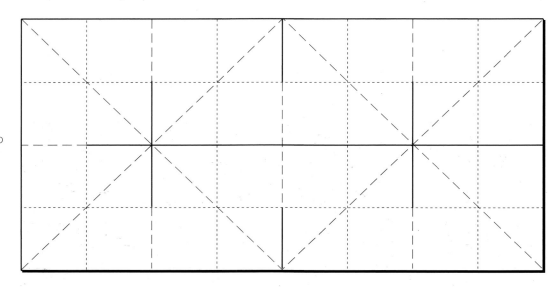

A diamond-fold maze book model reopened to show how the paper looks after folds and slits are made.

HAPPY BIRTHDAY, A DIAMOND-FOLD MAZE OR ORIGAMI BOOK BY MARY HOWE
PHOTO BY KEN WOISARD

Folded Exploding Cards

EXPLODING CARDS or invitations that pop out when you open them, combine origami and pop-up techniques. They are easy to make, by creating a diamond fold and adhering it, point up, to a piece of folded cardstock or to hard covers. Tuck confetti inside the card to add to the fun of opening it.

SIMPLE EXPLODING CARD

Begin folding a square of paper with the message side up (or create your message later). Make a horizontal valley fold and a vertical valley fold. Then flip the paper over and create a diagonal valley fold as shown on page 46. Push on the center of the fold to pop it into shape. Then adhere it to its backing with a dry adhesive.

ANOTHER IDEA

Multiples of the design, in graduated sizes, nested inside one another look exciting exploding from the interior of a book when its pages are opened. Just be sure that the center point of the explosion paper is flush with the spine of the book before you adhere the *unfolded* pages to two adjoining book pages. Once again, using a dry adhesive will give you best results.

A single diamond fold adhered to hinged bookboard makes a great pop-up party invitation. This invitation is by Jennifer Philippoff.

CREATING A FARMER'S PURSE EXPLODING CARD

WHAT YOU'LL NEED

Bone folder

Cardstock for card backing

Dry adhesive

Square of paper for the card

X-Acto knife and metal-edged ruler, or paper cutter

Although I'm not certain, I imagine that the term *farmer's purse* may have been coined by people using this simple paper structure to hold seeds being collected or sown.

Mary Howe, whose innovative cards and books are prized by the lucky people who receive them (and awed by those who view them), sent me this structure. Mary often uses it for her musical cards, like the "Happy Birthday" card pictured below.

The button on the front of the card activates a music box that plays a birthday song.

1 Creating the valley folds

To create a similar card, start with a square of paper facing you, right-side-up. Using the diagram on the opposite page as a reference, create a valley fold across each diagonal (A). Turn the paper over so that the wrong side is facing you and create a horizontal valley fold, as shown (B).

HAPPY BIRTHDAY 60TH, A FARMER'S PURSE EXPLODING CARD BY MARY HOWE
PHOTO BY KEN WOISARD

2 Creating the triangular structure

Pick up the paper so that the right side is facing you again, and push the center of the square slightly until the center pops outward. Then, using your index fingers, push the sides in to the center of the square creating the triangular structure shown (C). (*Note:* you will be looking at the wrong side of the paper or cardstock.)

3 Creasing the side flaps

Now fold each of the two side flaps forward to the center of the triangle (D & E) and backward to crease them in both directions. Flip the triangle over and do the same with the side flaps on the back of the structure.

4 Reverse-folding the side flaps

Reverse-fold the side flaps (F & G) that you previously creased.

5 Forming the final structure

Gently maneuver all folded flaps to form the structure pictured (H & I). The inside of the purse will feature the patterned or good side of your paper. It will show the fold lines evident in H and begin collapsing into figure I as you close it.

6 Finishing the card

To finish the card, create a cardstock or hard cover backing for your folded structure by cutting cardstock the same height as the original paper square and half the width. Use a dry adhesive to adhere the card together, making sure that the point at the top of the purse (when it is collapsed) lines up with the center of the folded cardstock.

ANOTHER IDEA

Collect some seeds from your favorite perennials, tuck them and a photo of your garden in bloom into an exploding card, and mail it to a friend.

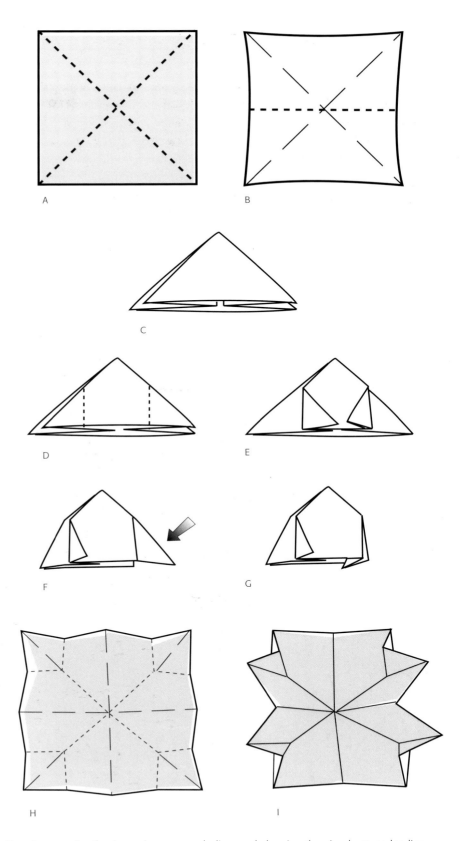

The diagrams for the farmer's purse exploding card showing the simple steps leading to Mary's delightful card.

Traditional Origami

ORIGAMI PAPER FOLDING, a familiar craft that you may have practiced as a child, can be used to create simple or sophisticated three-dimensional paper structures. Although the craft originated in China, the Japanese coined the term *origami* over a thousand years ago from the words *ori*, to fold, and *kami*, paper. The original

designers of many of the traditional designs, like the beautiful lilies shown below, are unknown. Although the same structures have been folded for centuries, each origami artist contributes his or her own personality by adjusting the folds in a unique way. The choice of the paper used to create the design will also influence the final design.

A bouquet of origami lilies created by Sandy Stern.

CREATING ORIGAMI LILIES

Sandy Stern, an accomplished paper artist well known for her fine craftsmanship, shares instructions for making her beautiful origami lilies shown on the opposite page. Refer to the illustration below showing the series of steps leading to the completed lily if you are unsure of what the model you are working on should look like. Traditional two-toned or patterned Japanese origami paper can be used, or you might try using wrapping paper or a thin decorated paper that holds a fold well.

1 Starting with a diamond fold

If the paper is single-sided, start with the wrong side up. Valley fold two opposite corners together, unfold, and repeat with the other two corners, to make a "plus sign" on the paper. Flip the paper over and fold and unfold the diagonals. Pick the paper up, and, from the wrong side, push on the center point so it "pops" out. Collapse the paper so it looks like a small square in (A).

2 Flattening the first flap

Holding the folded square with the center point of the original sheet downward lift up one of the flaps and flatten it so that the fold line matches up with the center opening underneath.

3 Flattening the remaining three flaps

Repeat the previous step with the other three flaps (C). (*Note:* Many times in this model, you will need to do the same thing on four sides. Do the front and back first, then fold those flaps in half to get to the other two sides.)

WHAT YOU'LL NEED

4 1/2-inch square piece of origami paper

18-gauge floral stem wire

Glue gun or tacky glue

Needle-nose pliers

Pencil

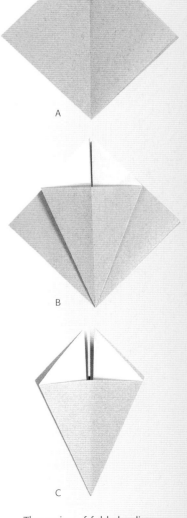

A

B

C

The series of folds leading to the completed lily.

After the paper is folded into figure A, begin flattening the flaps to arrive at figure B.

D

E

F

G

H

4 Folding the upper edges

On the front flap, fold the upper edges in to the center (D).

5 Pulling the center forward

Unfold the edges just folded and lift the center of the structure. Pull it toward you, easing the previous folds in again. As you lower the flap, fold the bottom of it from the side points to the center "squashing" it and creating a kite-shaped structure as shown emerging in the photo below center. Then fold the bottom point up toward the top of the structure (E). Repeat this last step on the remaining three flaps (F).

6 Creating the center of the lily

Fold one layer on the front and back of figure F over like the pages of a book to expose the inner solid surface and form a diamond-shaped structure (G). Then, on the front flap, fold the lower side edges to the center (H).

D

B

Figure B in the foreground has been completed. When all of the flaps have been similarly folded you'll arrive at figure C, shown being folded to reach figure D.

E

Lifting the lower portion of the figure D's flap to refold it into figure E. Repeat on the other three flaps to create figure F.

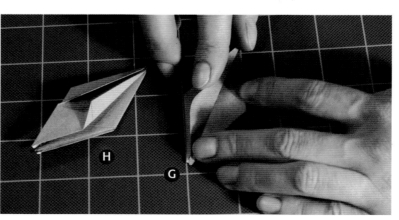

H

G

Find the interior flat plane by opening it like a book to reach figure G, then fold the edges in to complete the first step of figure H.

7 Folding down the first petal

Repeat step 6 on the other three places where the model has a solid surface and fold the first petal down to arrive at figure I.

8 Opening the lily

Fold each of the four petals down as far as they can go comfortably. This step is optional; it opens the lily up more. If you are making a bouquet of lilies, you may want to do some with the fold and some without, as shown in the arrangement on page 52.

9 Curling the petals

Starting at the tip, roll each petal around a pencil to curl it.

10 Applying the finishing touches

Use the pliers to make a small loop on the end of one wire stem. Carefully insert the wire inside the lily and poke it through the center of the bottom. Apply hot glue or tacky glue to the wire loop and pull the loop all the way into the flower and hold or hang the lily upside down until the glue is set.

When the folds for figure H are repeated on all four solid surfaces, you can begin folding the four petals down to reach figure I.

The lily with all four petals folded down. The figure on the left shows the same structure with the first petal folded down.

Curling the lily petals.

CREATING AN ORIGAMI BOWL AND LID

WHAT YOU'LL NEED

FOR THE BOWL

Decorative text weight
paper for bowl

Metal-edged ruler

Pencil

X-Acto knife

FOR THE LID

Bone folder

Bookboard

Decorative paper

Mat knife

Ruler

Scrap paper

Square

White glue and
glue brush

Debra Glanz has taken another traditional origami structure, the origami bowl, and with the addition of a fanciful tiered rigid top has transformed it into a charming lidded vessel. The owner of a paper company called Reminiscence Papers, she designs and markets her own patterned papers, which enhance the structures she creates—a marriage of paper folding and bookbinding techniques. When Debra combines several bowls in graduated sizes she creates sculptural towers (page 61). Debra's instructions for creating an origami bowl are below.

1 Dividing your paper into thirds

Begin with a sheet of decorative paper with a text weight of 20 to 32 pounds. Later, you can work with cardstock for more durable bowls. Cut your sheet of paper at a ratio of 2:3 (for example, 4 × 6 inches or 6 × 9 inches). On the right side of your paper make two small pencil marks along the longest edge, dividing your paper into thirds (A).

2 Folding along the thirds lines

Bring one short edge of your paper over to meet the pencil mark furthest from it (B). Crease. Open that fold (C) and repeat from the opposite side (D), leaving this side folded.

3 Folding the outer thirds in half

Bring the cut edge of the recently folded section back out to the folded edge (E). Crease. Repeat with the opposite side (F). At this point your paper has three layers. You will be looking at the right or decorated side of the paper.

The bowl with lid removed.

4 Folding the first four corners

Open one of your folded sides over the other (G). Bring the two cut corners down to meet the center fold line (H). Crease. Do the same with the two folded corners (I). (Depending on the weight of your paper, these may be a bit stiffer to fold.)

5 Folding the remaining corners

Return the cut edge to the outer folded edge leaving all four folded corners tucked inside. You'll see the right side of the paper again (J). Open the other folded side over the side with the tucked corners (K). Repeat steps 4 and 5 to fold down all four corners and return the cut edge to the folded one (L, M, & N).

6 Opening the bowl

Finally, grasp the center of each of the inside folds. Gently pull up and out, being careful not to pull too hard and cause the layers at the points to separate. Keep pulling these folds until they nearly lie flat. "Squash" and crease the unit, making two new points (O).

7 Shaping the bowl

From the outside, gently squeeze the two points of this unit allowing it to pop into a bowl shape (P). You may help this step along by prodding and pulling where necessary.

DECORATIVE LID

You can easily create a lid to fit any size origami bowl using the same techniques you used to create the accordion-fold book covers.

1 Constructing the lid

Measure the bottom of your origami bowl and then transfer the measurements to a piece of bookboard or heavy matboard. Make sure that the grain of your board runs vertically. Use a mat knife and a ruler or a heavy-duty paper cutter to cut out two boards to make the two-part cover for your

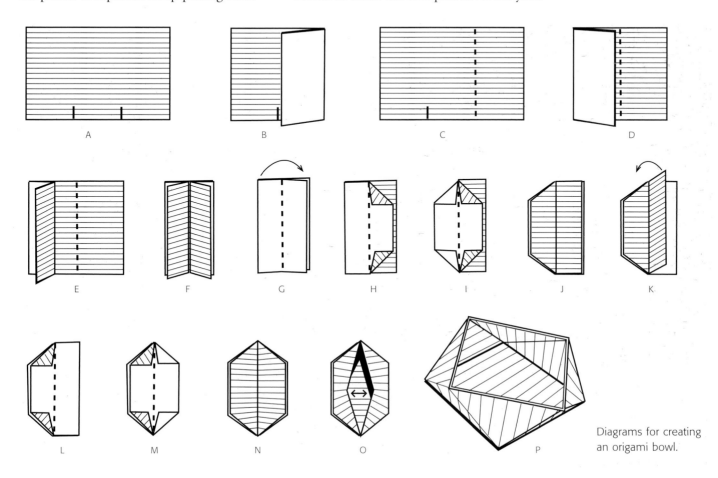

Diagrams for creating an origami bowl.

bowl. One board should be 1 inch wider and longer than the base of the bowl, or 4 inches square for a bowl with a 3-inch square base. The second piece of board should be cut $1/8$-inch smaller all around than the bowl base, corresponding to the bowl's opening. (When they are eventually glued together, the smaller board will rest inside the bowl to keep the lid in place.)

2 Finessing your work

Check to be sure that the corners are cut at right angles and that edges are straight. If the cutting has left ragged edges on your board, lightly sand them.

TIP

Although matching grain direction may not be essential for working with tiny bowl lids, larger ones may warp if grain direction is not matched.

3 Preparing the cover papers

A fanciful origami bowl by Debra Glanz.

Check for grain direction on the text weight decorative paper you've chosen to cover the bookboard. Arrange it on your worktable so that the grain matches your bookboard and then cut two pieces, each 1 inch wider and longer than the bowl covers. This will allow for a $1/2$-inch border around each cover board.

Cover each piece of bookboard following the directions of page 42. When both boards are covered, glue them together with the wrong side of the smaller paper-covered board centered on the wrong side of the larger one and place under a heavy weight until the glue is dry.

ANOTHER IDEA

If you want to stitch buttons, beads, or a tassel to decorate the bowl lid, punch stitching holes with an awl and hide the stitching material between the lid liner and the bowl cover before they are glued together. Additional thinner boards in graduated sizes could also be added to decorate the bowl lid, or beads could be glued in place with jeweler's cement. A platform can also be created for the origami bowl by covering bookboard and gluing it to the base of the bowl.

Gallery Tour

LEFT *WASPS AS PAPERMAKERS*
(3 × 3½ × 3½ INCHES) BY MARY HOWE
In addition to handmade paper, this accordion-fold book contains wasp nest paper, Canson Mi-Teintes paper, and mica. The text on the piece was excerpted from an article in *Good Literature* printed in 1908. Photo by Ken Woisard.

BELOW ORIGAMI BOXES
(2½ × 2 × 2 INCHES) BY CLAUDIA LEE
Claudia's handmade paper boxes sport a variety of beads and buttons used to decorate and tie them closed. A classic origami kimono artfully decorates the fold-over panel of some of her boxes while others perch on paper-wrapped wooden feet. Claudia often further decorates her colorful handmade papers by Xeroxing designs on top of them.

CONGRATULATIONS (3 × 3 INCHES, CLOSED), A MAZE BOOK BY MARY HOWE
Mary creates many types of maze books, but all are based on the concept of folding and then cutting parts of the folds to open a single piece of paper that is then manipulated into a book. Finding your way through the twists and turns of the emerging book structure is a bit like finding your way through a maze. Photo by Ken Woisard.

FANTASY GARDENS (4³/₄ × 38 INCHES, OPENED) BY DIANE MAURER-MATHISON
This accordion-fold book holds six dimensional paper collages on its heavy watercolor paper pages. The collages are created with mat board, commercial paper, handmade paper, and the author's marbled paper, paste paper, and orizomegami fold and dye designs.

FACETED TOWER (6 × 18 INCHES) BY DEBRA GLANZ

Individual origami bowls take on a new artful dimension when they are stacked together to become a tower. The papers used are all designed and produced by Debra's wholesale paper company, Reminiscence Papers.

CHAPTER 3

Constructing
PAPER
POP-UPS

PAPER POP-UPS, surprises that appear as if by magic when a sheet of paper is opened out, folded down, flipped up or otherwise manipulated, are among the most entertaining dimensional paper art projects. They are fun to make and receive, reawakening the child in all of us, which is why so many paper artists like Carol Barton, Constance Dawley, and others are continuing to explore the genre. A good way to experience pop-ups and see what commercial "paper engineers" are doing is to visit the children's section of a large bookstore. Elaborate multilevel mansions complete with furniture pop up when book pages are lifted, and denizens of the deep swimming through seaweed gardens arise when tabs are pulled. I know several adults, including my daughter, who are avid pop-up book collectors. (One of my favorites is the very scary *Pop-up Book of Phobias*.)

Although there is not room to explore pop-ups in great detail in this book, this chapter will give you an introduction to simple pop-ups and have you creating your own in a few minutes. You don't even have to like math to proceed. Books with pop-up pages and foldout panels; cards that contain ledges, steps, and amazing architectural details; sculptural forms that collapse flat with a twist of the wrist; and pop-up costumes created for performance art are some of the delights that await you in this chapter.

OPPOSITE *HOME DREAMS* BY CAROL BARTON

Shown are two pages from one of Carol's accordion books, playful looks at peoples' views of their ideal home. The book was created during her own renovation project. *Home Dreams* features five small pop-up houses that overlie a text listing comments on various living situations.

Pop-Up Basics

POP-UPS SHOULD BE a fun—for the creator as well as the viewer. But many students, I find, are intimidated by the prospect of trying to create a pop-up. They're afraid of the math and measuring required. It is true that if pop-up measurements and folds are off, it will be obvious. In addition, if you have overhandled a paper trying to determine which folds recess and which protrude, that will also be evident in the finished pop-up. For this reason, I always suggest designing prototypes of simple pop-ups on inexpensive graph paper first, so you can determine where to cut and how to fold before you make the finished work on stiffer more expensive paper.

VISION SHIFTS, A POP-UP BOOK BY CAROL BARTON

Constance Dawley has used the pop-up step as a support for parallel bars for her jumping frogs in her amusing book page. Notice how the tabs from the bars attach to the pop-up step allowing the bars to fold when the bottom of the page is folded back up.

To begin playing with pop-ups, buy a tablet of graph paper laid out with four squares to the inch. With only a sheet of graph paper and a pair of scissors you can create pop-ups in minutes—without measuring a thing.

1 Making the graph paper practice sheet

To make a step or a pop-up support for a paper cutout, just fold a sheet of graph paper in half and, near the center of the sheet, make two slits, as illustrated in the top image below. The slits shown are seven squares deep and a couple of inches apart. Cut them following a graph paper line and be sure to end each cut at the bottom of the same square. Your slits should be even *and* parallel. Fold and crease the flap of paper you just created along the dotted line that connects the base of each slit. Move it backward and then forward to crease it in both directions.

2 Pushing the flap through to create a step

Now open your folded paper enough to push the flap through to the other side and flatten it. The top of the flap, which was originally a mountain fold, will become a valley fold. Use a bone folder to sharpen the paper creases. Now open the paper to see a little step that, when made on heavier paper, can be used as a pop-up support for an image. Parts of the step can also be cut away to create a more detailed pop-up design. If the paper is turned on its side, the step you just made can become a little window (if pushed in) or a blocklike projection.

WHAT YOU'LL NEED
Bone folder
Cardstock or cover stock
Graph paper
Pin
Metal ruler
Scissors
X-Acto knife

BELOW Joan B. Machinchick's *Seasons of the Bay—Splendor* shows how part of the pop-up step can be reversed to become a little recessed window.

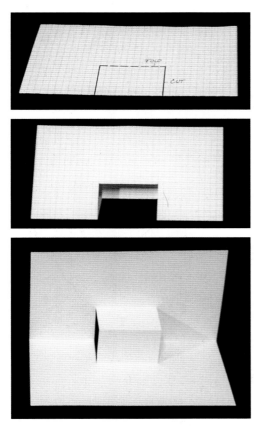

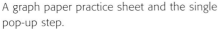
A graph paper practice sheet and the single pop-up step.

3 Creating two more steps

To make two more steps, cut two more slits, each two squares in from the first ones. Make these about three squares deep and follow the same procedure as before to fold the paper in both directions and reverse the folds by pushing the flaps through. Your paper will look like the second part of the illustration below when it's flat. When opened, it will sport three steps or ledges that, when made of heavier paper, can be decorated with drawings or collage work. Turn the paper on its side again to see the beginnings of an interesting architectural design. The book by Ruth Ann Petree (bottom) shows a variation of this design with folds reversed or steps pushed in.

4 Transferring graph-paper designs to heavy paper

Cardstock or a cover stock, like Canson Mi-Teintes, are good papers to use for the finished pop-ups. The papers are thin enough to crease with light scoring and rigid enough to hold the crease. To transfer your practice sheet to heavier paper without measuring, place the design over the paper, making sure the fold lines *follow* the grain. Prick the paper with a pin to mark the end of each slit, connect the pin marks with a metal ruler, and cut parallel slits. You can repeatedly use your graph-paper designs as patterns. *Note:* When working with very heavy paper, you will need to score the base of flaps before attempting to crease and reverse their folds.

Triple pop-up steps and the graph paper practice sheet used to make them.

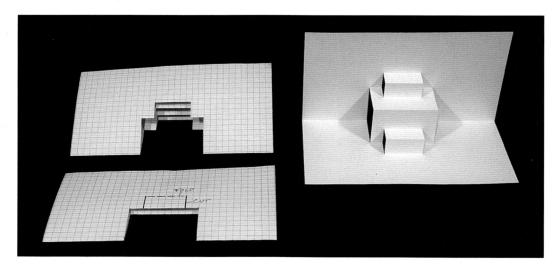

A book by Ruth Ann Petree featuring a reverse variation of the pop-up step design.

ANOTHER IDEA

Cut a series of parallel slits like those shown in the illustration at right. Before opening the paper, bend each narrow flap forward and then backwards to crease it. Then carefully reverse the folds by pulling each flap to the front. Then close the paper again and crease the flaps into their final positions. The pop-up fish by Hal Lose shows how the same technique can be slightly altered to produce representational designs.

A SIMPLE POP-UP CARD

A pop-up card, with a central area that is reverse folded to pop-up when the card is opened, is based on the same principle as a pop-up step. To make a card, draw, trace, or stamp a design in the center of a piece of paper whose central fold line matches the paper's grain. Cut around the design, using an X-Acto knife over a self-healing cutting mat, leaving the *edges* of the design attached to the paper. Then reverse the fold, bringing the valley-folded center of the design forward to transform it into a mountain fold.

APPLYING POP-UP STEPS IN BOOK AND CARD DESIGNS

Many successful pop-up designs have their basis in very simple structures like the steps just shown. Carol Barton, an internationally acclaimed book artist and paper engineer, used pop-up steps in her witty and beautiful *Alphabetica Synthetica.* She notes that a successful piece is not defined by technique alone, and stresses that the visual themes, typography, and color schemes are as important as the architecture of the page. When Carol designs a piece, she creates a series of visual models and sketches. She may make a quick paper-engineering test with a scrap of paper, but then proceeds to a series of as many as forty increasingly complex models before she is satisfied with a design. Her workbook *The Pocket Paper Engineer*, published by her company Popular Kinetics Press, is a great book for learning basic pop-up mechanisms and how to adapt forms to your own artistic motifs.

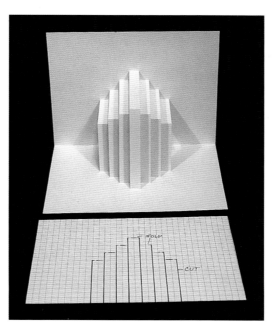

LEFT A pop-up featuring multiple slits and its graph paper practice sheet.
BELOW A pop-up fish by Hal Lose employing the multiple slit technique.

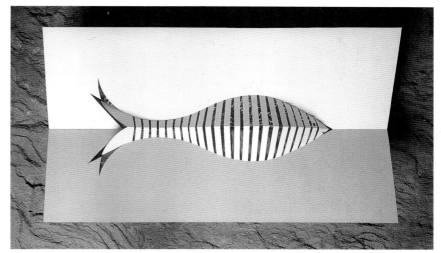

ALPHABETICA SYNTHETICA BY CAROL BARTON

Pop-Up Flag Books

THE FLAG BOOK, sometimes called a winged accordion-fold book, holds surprises between its covers. The book has an accordion-folded center spine on which strips of paper are attached. When the book cover is opened, instead of finding traditional pages, the viewer sees many flaglike, narrow pages popping out in opposing directions. The pages can hold stamped or stenciled images, photographs, famous quotations, or samples of decorative papers to produce a kind of specimen book.

Flag book pages can be made in many ways. Constance Dawley used rubber-stamped cutouts to create humorous pages for her flag book, *Saturday Night Frog Hop at the Pond*.

Flag book pages can be encased in conventional hard or soft covers. They can also be nestled between covers shaped and colored to resemble a trout to relate to the theme of the book, as here in *The Catch* by Constance Dawley.

CREATING A SIMPLE FLAG BOOK

I used some handmade paper stationery to create the flag book below. The notepaper colors were so vibrant, I decided they needed no further decoration. I did a bit of collage on the covers, however, in homage to the envelopes that came with the set.

1 Making the accordion spine

Using a bone folder, crease the 6 × 8-inch (h × w) strip of paper in half, then fold in each end to meet the center fold. This folds the paper into quarters. Next, fold the cut edges back to the folded ones. Keep the paper folded and turn the paper over. Align and crease the folded ends with the center fold. You will now have an accordion spine with alternating mountain and valley folds at 1-inch intervals.

Thick or rigid papers are difficult to fold neatly without scoring them first and tend to crack if you fold in the wrong direction and then try to reverse the fold to fix them. If you find that this technique doesn't work

with the paper you've selected, try the following alternate method of scoring your paper on the correct side before accordion-folding it.

Begin by positioning your paper so that the front faces you and fold the paper in half. Now flip the paper over and, working on the back of the paper, measure out 2 inches from the right side of the center score line (which is a mountain fold when viewed from the back) and make a depression in your paper with the tip of the awl. Do the same on the left side of the center score line. Score the paper on the back of the project at each mark. Then flip the paper over so the front faces you.

To score on this side of the paper, mark off the two lines that fall between the previous folds at 1-inch marks. Score and then fold the accordion "spine" of your flag book. Your folds will all be going in the correct direction, and the spine should easily fall into pleats.

WHAT YOU'LL NEED

One 6 × 8-inch piece of paper (short grain for easy folding) for the accordion-folded spine

Two 6 × 8 1/2-inch papers for the book covers

Fifteen 1 × 4-inch flag pages

Bone folder

Canson Mi-Teintes drawing paper, handmade paper, or another sturdy paper that folds easily

Glue or dry adhesive

A flag book.

2 Creating and attaching the covers

Take the two $6 \times 8\,^1/_2$-inch pieces, which will become your soft covers, and fold them in half so that the "good" side is facing out. Apply glue or dry adhesive to the end tab of the accordion-folded spine and adhere one inside edge of the folded cover as shown. Then apply adhesive around the remaining inside edges of the folded cover to create a double-layered cover and simultaneously adhere the cover to the back of the spines' end tab. Repeat to create a cover for the other side of the book. I decorated the inside of the covers of the flag book (pictured below) with layered paper triangles to add to the fun when the book is opened.

3 Creating the flag pages

The flag pages are mounted on opposing sides of the mountain folds that appear when the book is opened. Nine 1×4-inch flags will be adhered to the left-hand sides of the accordion-folds. These will swing open to the right when the book is opened. Six flags will be mounted on the right hand sides of the folds and swing to the left when the book is opened. Cut and decorate each flag page if desired, and set it aside. (For your first book, you may just want to work with colored paper strips that you can punch or collage onto later.)

4 Gluing the flag pages in place

To prepare for gluing the flags in place, measure and mark 1 inch into each flag (the width of each side of the mountain folds). This will tell you where to apply the glue or dry adhesive. Adhere one set of flags to the left side of each of the spine's mountain folds. Line two flags up $^1/_{16}$-inch in from the top and bottom edges of the book, and center an additional flag between the two outer ones. Then glue the other set of flags in place on the right-hand side of each mountain fold, making sure that they are placed in such a way as to swing through the other flags when the book is opened.

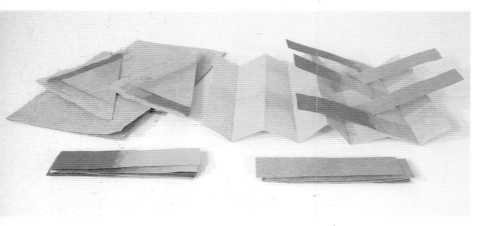

ABOVE Gluing the flags in place on the accordion-folded spine.
RIGHT The flag book with pages in place and one cover partially attached.

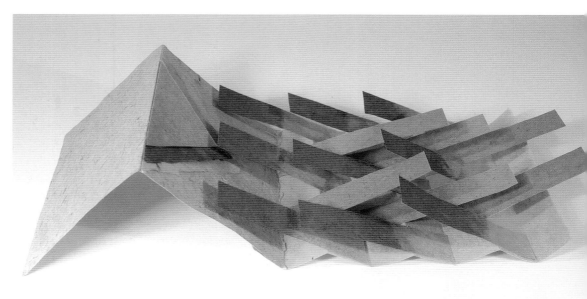

Origamic Architecture

TWO DECADES AGO, Japanese professor/ architect Masahiro Chatani was inspired by origami to create a new dimensional paper art form called "origamic architecture." By cutting and folding a single piece of paper, he replicated architectural details of buildings around the world. Some ten years later, Ingrid Siliakus, a Dutch artist, saw the work of Professor Chatani and was fascinated by the ingenious manner in which his origamic architecture cards were designed—and by the beauty they radiated. After studying Professor Chatani's art for some years, she began creating her own designs. Ingrid's specialties are buildings of master architects (she was recently commissioned by the Museum of Modern Art in New York to create a work replicating the redesigned museum building) and intricate abstract sculptures inspired by the works of artists like M. C. Escher.

Ingrid believes that the art form is not really origami, as precision *cutting* is essential to creating origamic architecture works. (True origami is made only by folding paper.) Some people think origamic architecture has its roots more in pop-ups. But that label is not wholly accurate either. As Ingrid explains, "The distinction between pop-up cards and paper (origamic) architecture cards is that in pop-up cards a model is usually folded out of more sequences of paper. With paper (origamic) architecture, however, an object is cut out of a single piece of paper. It is done by a combination of detailed cutting and folding. To design a pattern from scratch, the artist needs the skills of an architect to create a two-dimensional design, which with the patience and precision of a surgeon, becomes an ingenious three-dimensional wonder of paper."

The word *card*, I must say, seems totally inappropriate when used to describe Ingrid's work. Her reversed mirror image designs are on a par with those of the finest paper artists. I do see a relation to pop-ups, however, and hope that the previous exercises will give you the confidence to try your hand at origamic architecture.

REFLECTION BY INGRID SILIAKUS
This masterful work in origamic architecture was inspired by the work of artist M. C. Escher. The bottom half is an exact mirror image of the top, only flipped horizontally.

CREATING THE CANAL HOUSE CARD

WHAT YOU'LL NEED

Cardstock
Bamboo skewer or dowel
Dry adhesive
Dull knife blade (optional)
Eraser
Metal ruler
Pencil
Removable tape
Self-healing cutting mat
Stylus
X-Acto knife

Ingrid Siliakus believes that cutting and folding some cards from existing patterns is the best way to get an understanding of the craft. To help you become familiar with origamic architecture she has provided easy-to-follow instructions and a diagram for making *Canal House*, an origamic architecture card (pictured on page 74).

1 Copying the design

Place a sheet of cardstock on a cutting mat and draw a faint pencil line in the middle of each side of the paper. Draw it horizontally, matching the paper's grain. Copy the design by tracing it or scanning it into your computer and printing it out. Cut the copy paper down so that it fits on top of the cardstock, then attach it to the cardstock with removable tape, making sure that the midlines match up.

2 Perforating the cutting and folding lines

Mark all cutting and folding lines by making a tiny hole with a sharp stylus at the beginnings and the ends of the lines. The solid lines are the cutting lines. Lines made up of dashes, are the valley folds, and the dotted lines indicate mountain folds.

After all the lines have been carefully marked, remove the copy from the cardstock and erase the pencil lines. A completely perforated design will now appear on the cardstock.

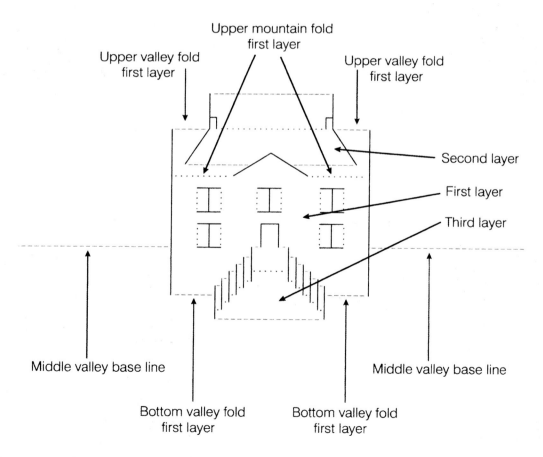

Upper mountain fold first layer

Upper valley fold first layer

Upper valley fold first layer

Second layer

First layer

Third layer

Middle valley base line

Middle valley base line

Bottom valley fold first layer

Bottom valley fold first layer

- - - - Valley folds
· · · · · Mountain folds
——— Cut lines

The *Canal House* diagram.

3 Cutting the solid lines

With the design as a guide, first cut the uninterrupted solid lines. Use a metal ruler and a sharp cutting knife, and cut from the beginning to the end of the line. Keep the knife perpendicular and try to cut the lines without pausing. Any hesitation or interruption will show in the piece.

4 Partially cutting or scoring the fold lines

The next step is to cut the fold lines two thirds of the way into the paper. You can also score deeply along these lines, but cutting is preferred. As before, make one straight cut, using the ruler as a guide from beginning to end. The valley folds are cut first, on the *back* of the cardstock. If you have never partially cut paper this way before, practice first on a separate piece of paper. You may also choose to reserve a special knife for partial cutting that is duller than your regular knife blade.

5 Folding the architecture card into shape

This step takes a lot of time and patience. Start by folding the middle valley base line (main fold line) to see which mountain folds move forward and appear by themselves when this is done. If some of the folds resist falling into place, you can score or cut them a bit more. Tweezers, or thin wooden dowels can be used to raise parts of the design and ease the mountain and valley folds into place. Do not try to position the folds all at once, but gently bend all of them a little and progress slowly.

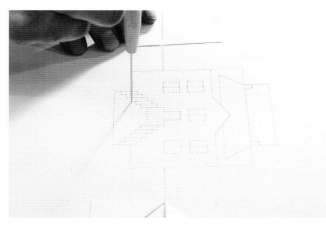
Perforating the cutting and folding lines.

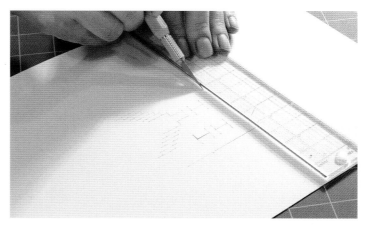
Cutting the solid lines.

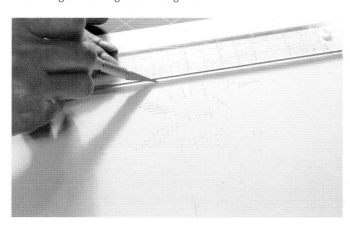
Partially cutting the fold lines.

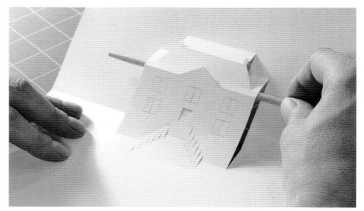
Using a wooden dowel to help raise part of the canal house and ease its mountain and valley folds into place.

Remember that the folds that are deeper get more difficult to reach as the card slowly finds its form. When all parts of the cards have been folded far enough, carefully close the card entirely. Use a bone folder to sharpen the folds.

Finally, you can adhere the cardstock to another heavier piece of paper if you desire. If you created your card from a heavy piece of cardstock, it may not be necessary to glue it to another piece of paper.

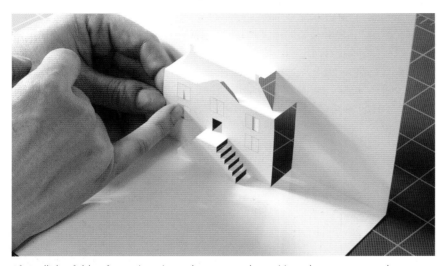

After all the folds of an origamic card are properly positioned you can attend to details like opening the tiny windows of a structure.

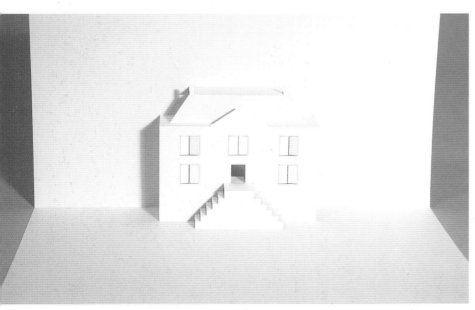

CANAL HOUSE BY INGRID SILIAKUS

DESIGNING YOUR OWN CARD

When you have completed Ingrid's *Canal House* you may want to try designing your own card. I asked Ingrid how someone could best go about creating a simple design. She stressed that one should (as she did) start with cutting and folding as many cards as possible from existing patterns to get a solid understanding of origamic architecture. Look for Ingrid's book *Origamic Architecture from Building to Card* along with other books containing origamic architecture patterns.

When designing a card, she noted, the most important line is the middle base fold line—a valley fold—as shown in the diagram on page 72. The best thing to do is use graph paper and put the horizontal middle base line in first. If you wish to recreate an actual house, photographs should be taken from all angles to see which side of the structure would be best for the design. When you have decided which part of the house you will use, you divide the house in layers. You start by drawing one layer onto your graph paper, with the middle line as your guide. The cut lines are drawn vertically and the fold lines horizontally.

The measurement from the bottom horizontal valley fold to the middle base line should be exactly the same as the upper mountain fold line is to the upper valley fold line. Next, the second layer is drawn onto the first layer, using the bottom valley fold of the first layer as your guide. You now do the same with the second layer as you did with the first layer. And then you proceed to the next layer, and so on.

When you are done, Ingrid adds, you scan the design into the computer and print it out, or photocopy it, and cut and fold it to see how it works. When you are satisfied with the basics of the house, you draw the windows, doors, and other decorations.

Slice-Form Pop-Ups

ANOTHER TYPE of dimensional paper art popularized by Masahiro Chatani is often referred to as "geometric origami." According to a leading practitioner of the craft, Sandy Jackson, it really has little to do with origami and is more appropriately called "slice forms." In slice forms, three-dimensional models of various objects are created by fitting together slices of paper inserted into a series of slots to create the form. When the structure is standing open, the slices are at right angles to one another. When the paper angles are decreased, the form begins to collapse and eventually lays flat. Slice forms have been used for many years to make mathematical models.

Sandy's interest in slice forms (she admits a lifelong interest in puzzles and geometry, so she probably *likes* math) began when she took Masahiro Chatani's book *Pop-Up Geometric Origami* along on a trip to Paris. Before she was able to tackle any of the projects in the book, however, Sandy was overcome by the desire to make a model of the Eiffel Tower. She followed that successful project with a pop-up slice-form tree for a Christmas card. Before long she was designing and selling kits to make various slice-form structures and selling pattern stamps to decorate the forms through her business SAS (Some Assembly Required).

Slice-form pears by Sandy Jackson.

CREATING A SLICE-FORM EIFFEL TOWER

WHAT YOU'LL NEED

Cover stock

Graph paper

Matboard

Scissors

Stylus

X-Acto knife with
#11 blade or craft knife

When I asked Sandy how to design a slice form from scratch, she gave the following directions for creating an Eiffel Tower. You can use these as a guide to create your own designs. Making designs with Sandy's kits can also help you get a feel for how objects like a pear or egg might be replicated in paper slices. Many of the steps could be done on the computer, but paper artists may prefer to create the structure the "old fashioned way."

Sandy explains, "I use either a real object or a picture of an object to get some key measurements to establish some reference points and get the basic shape." For the Eiffel Tower project she used a postcard of the monument and drew the structure on graph paper.

1 Making a set of templates

Since the Eiffel Tower needs multiples of some pieces, you need to make a set of templates. To make a set of templates, lay the graph paper on top of a piece of cover stock with a piece of matboard underneath. Use a stylus to poke holes through the graph paper and cover stock to position the corners, curves, and slots.

Next, cut out the template pieces, leaving a border around each shape so that the holes aren't too close to the edge of the paper, which would make the shape unstable.

2 Transferring the pattern

Then repeat the hole-poking process to transfer the pattern to the final piece of paper. There are two different tower top sections, two sets of four identical pieces for the middle, and the bottom (legs) of the tower. Most sections of the structure can be cut with a craft knife, but the slots should be cut with scissors.

Drawing the Eiffel Tower model from a photographic reference.

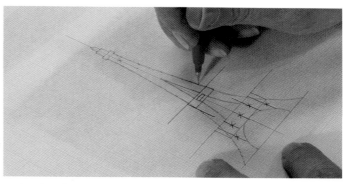

Perforating the graph paper drawing and the red coverstock beneath it to begin creating a pattern for a tower section.

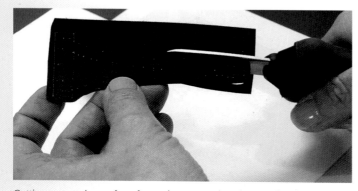

Cutting out a piece of perforated coverstock to be used as a template.

Using the template to perforate the orange paper used for the tower.

3 Cutting the slots

The slots, at this point, are really a thin line of holes, marking the area to be cut. The width of the slots ($^1/_{32}$- to $^3/_{32}$-inch wide) will be easier to maintain if cut with scissors rather than using a knife and a straightedge. When using scissors, cut along the right edge of the slot and end the cut by closing the scissors. Then cut along the left edge of the slot in the same way. A sliver of paper will usually curl down a bit and stick out below the main piece of paper. Remove the sliver by turning the paper 90 degrees counterclockwise. Then use the tip of the scissors to cut across the end (just like cutting any inside corner). Resist the temptation to turn the paper over when cutting the end of the slot. If you cut from the back, the cutting edge of the scissors will be $^1/_6$-inch away from the end of the sliver. This will always leave a little piece of paper at the end of the slot, which will get in the way when you put the model together.

Cutting out a tower section.

Creating a slot in a tower section.

The tower parts ready to be assembled.

4 Assembling the tower

After all the slots are cut, carefully fit the tower's sections together according to the diagram below. When fully assembled, a twist of the wrist will collapse the slice form so that it is flat enough to send through the mail. A recipient can then easily pop it up again into a small freestanding sculpture.

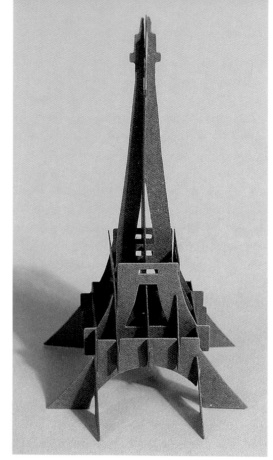

The Eiffel Tower slice form by Sandy Jackson.

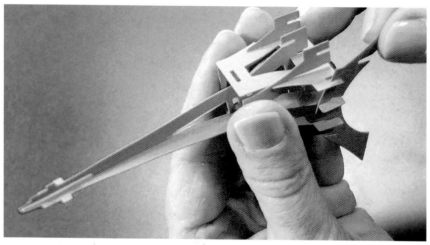

Assembling the tower by fitting the slots together.

The tower diagram.

Wearable Pop-Ups

SUSAN SHARE'S POP-UP BOOKS are actually sculptural costumes meant to be worn and artfully manipulated in a kind of dance as she interacts with each structure in performance art. The colors, patterns, and motion of Susan's dance as she unfolds and animates her art, transforming it from one amazing creaturelike structure into another, is riveting. I know, since I was fortunate enough to see one of her performances some years ago. The lethal looking pop-up spikes that suddenly emerge from some of her wearable art pieces are particularly arresting—delighting a viewer and yet sending shivers up your spine at the same time.

The photographs below show *Box for a Brighter Side* at various stages of its transformation as it is used in performance. Susan explains, "In its closed suitcaselike form it is wheeled around on a dolly by the performer. As it opens, it spreads outward, upward, and across the floor, and may be arranged in various configurations. Contained within its folds are both the set and costume for this visual art performance."

Susan uses many box and folder construction methods as well as pop-up techniques in her sculptural books, many of which she learned during her studies of traditional bookbinding and conservation. She starts by painting 4 × 6-foot sheets of paper with acrylic paint and then cuts and reconfigures the paintings and other collage materials in her foldout and pop-up structures. *Brooklyn Bridge Resuspended* is from what she calls her "spike phase." To create such a work, she explains, "I paint papers, cut the desired spike shape, create a folder, and glue in successive pop-up pieces. Each pop-up has a cloth loop or two on the outside for attachment to hands or to facilitate opening."

BROOKLYN BRIDGE RESUSPENDED, A PERFORMANCE ART POP-UP BY SUSAN JOY SHARE
The piece was created by painting, cutting, and folding paper elements.

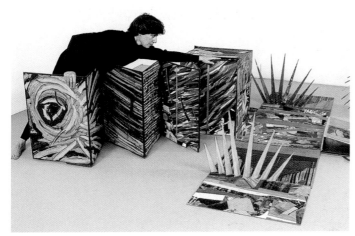

Susan Joy Share opening her *Box for a Brighter Side*, which holds the set and the pop-up costumes for her visual art performance.

Box for a Brighter Side, shown completely open. Photos by Doug Beube.

Gallery Tour

THROUGH THE LOOKING GLASS (3¹/₂ × 4³/₄ × 1¹/₄ INCHES, OPENS TO 35 INCHES) BY CONSTANCE DAWLEY

This flag book, inspired by Lewis Carroll's *Alice in Wonderland*, is made from mirror and metallic finish paper, in addition to black-and-white and color illustrations and matboard. Note how the checkerboard paper lining the rigid covers echoes the repetitive pattern of the flag pages.

SEASONS OF THE BAY—MIDSUMMER GIFT (5¹/₂ × 25 INCHES, OPENED) BY JOAN B. MACHINCHICK

This work is a soft-cover double-accordion-fold pop-up book. Its slits allow a second set of pages to be passed through them. The photography, poetry, and calligraphy are all done by Joan.

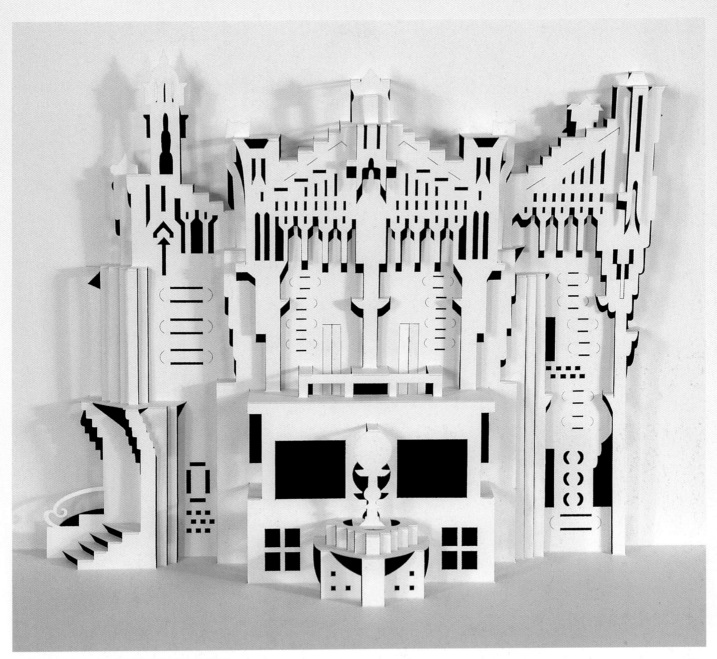

CASA VICENS (8 × 11¹/₂ INCHES) BY INGRID SILIAKUS
Ingrid's meticulous attention to detail is especially evident in this particularly intricate piece of origamic architecture. It was inspired by the single-family residence Casa Vicens, designed by Antoni Gaudí. "Seeking and finding a cooperation with each type of paper and with each cut or fold one makes," Ingrid notes, "is an immensely fascinating and challenging process."

CHAPTER 4

Exploring
TRADITIONAL
PAPER SCULPTURE

TRADITIONAL PAPER SCULPTURE, sometimes called three-dimensional illustration, has a long history as a medium employed by illustrators and graphic designers for use in advertising. It most often focuses on realistic subject matter as opposed to abstract designs like those shown in the work of Jeanne Petrosky (see chapter 1). Once used in store window displays to attract shoppers' attention, three-dimensional illustration soon gravitated to magazines and newspapers where in 1932 it was even used to sell Ivory soap. Today, although still used extensively in advertising, traditional paper sculpture is now receiving its proper respect as a fine arts medium and finding its place in galleries worldwide. It is a fun medium to explore, and because you can copy source materials to create works rather than having to be a skilled draftsman, with a little practice most anyone can produce simple paper sculptures.

Paper sculpture is sometimes defined as paper that has been transformed from a flat plane into a three-dimensional form with concave and convex surfaces. Light and shadow play on these surfaces to create dramatic visual effects. If you crumple a white piece of paper, place it near a lamp and take a moment to observe the hills and valleys created, you'll see how light paints the various paper planes in varying degrees and shades of shadow. Many paper sculptors, like David Wood, prefer to work with stark white paper for it's dramatic effect, while others like to make more colorful works, often creating their own decorative papers to use in their art.

OPPOSITE *LA TIMES CULTURE* BY HAL LOSE

An Introduction to Paper Sculpture

MUCH CAN BE LEARNED about paper sculpture by cutting out different paper shapes and bending or curling them to see what kinds of forms can be created. Ideas for paper sculptures may grow from your experiments as you realize that by scoring and shaping a narrow pointed piece of paper you've created a structure that closely resembles pond grass or by rolling oval-shaped cutouts over a pencil you've created realistic columbine flower petals. Work with white medium-weight paper when you begin. Then try papers in various weights to familiarize yourself with their possibilities.

COLUMBINE (DETAIL)
BY NANCY LENORE COOK
Although Nancy typically works with Canson and other western papers, the background in this sculpture is a Japanese paper called Kyoseishi. Nancy uses colored papers in many of her works and enjoys the way the subtleties and shadings of colors mimic those in nature.

CREATING BASIC PAPER SCULPTURE ELEMENTS

Some of the techniques used in paper sculpture—cutting, scoring, and creating mountain and valley folds—are discussed on pages 36–39. By learning a few more techniques, such as curling, rolling, and feathering, you'll soon be able to shape paper into three-dimensional curved structures.

Making an S-shape

Begin exploring three-dimensional curved shapes by using an X-Acto knife to cut out an elongated S-shape from a piece of heavy paper. If using machine-made paper, be sure the S follows the grain of the paper. Then use an X-Acto knife with a dull blade or a stylus to score the cutout, following the curve down the center of the S. (You can try using the same blade you used to cut out the S-shape but apply minimal pressure to avoid cutting completely through the paper.) Now create a mountain fold, using your fingers, to bend the sheet away

from the scored line. The resulting form will be a curved shape with angular flat planes that catch and reflect the light. This shape could represent ripples in a pond or stream.

Exploring other curved shapes

Cut out a wider piece of paper and try scoring two curving lines in it—one on the front of the sheet to be bent into a mountain fold and one on the reverse side of the sheet to become a valley fold. Now try slicing out more narrow, slightly curved pieces of paper that taper to a point. Score and fold these to create new structures that could become elements for a paper sculpture.

TIP

Although you may be tempted to try cutting shapes with scissors, long gentle curves can be most accurately cut with a sharp X-Acto knife.

WHAT YOU'LL NEED

Medium-weight white paper (such as Canson Mi-Teintes)

Self-healing cutting mat

Glue brush

Paper curling devices (a wooden dowel and bone folder will be fine)

Stylus

Toothpicks (these can be used to apply glue in areas too small for glue brush application)

White glue

X-Acto knife with #11 blades (a second knife with a dull blade will be helpful)

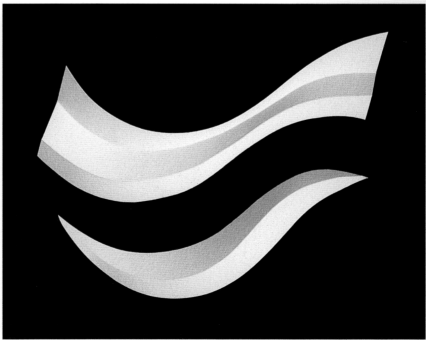

LEFT Bending the scored paper away from the fold line to create a mountain fold.
ABOVE The angular flat planes of scored and raised paper catch and reflect light.

Mastering curled paper

To practice curling paper, cut out a long strip of paper with the grain running across it, and roll it over the edge of a bone folder as though you're curling a ribbon for a gift package. Now roll an identical piece of paper around a dowel to see how that influences curl. Notice how much the paper springs back. Think about how curled forms might be used in a piece to represent flower tendrils cascading from a bouquet or curls of hair peeking out from under a woman's hat. Play with the forms to see how they can be further shaped by rolling them with your fingers to tighten them, or by pulling the paper to open a curl. Try curling different kinds and weights of paper to see how each reacts.

Making circular or oval shapes

Cut out a paper circle or teardrop shape and slice into its center. Overlap the edges and glue one edge over the other to create a structure that might become a flower petal, a horseshoe crab shell, or, if divided at the top and the bottom with smooth flowing cuts as in Hal Lose's sun sculpture (below), the beginnings of an animated face. Another way to give a flat cutout a rounded shape is to use a metal spoon burnisher (used for transfer lettering and metal crafts) over a soft surface. Australian calligrapher and paper sculptor David Wood notes that it is critical that each cutout be shaped around all of the edges on the back of the paper to take the sharpness off the paper and give a rounded effect.

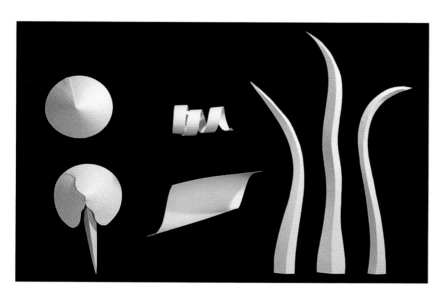

ABOVE Scored and curled papers can become elements for many different paper sculptures.

RIGHT *SUN IMAGE* BY HAL LOSE

Paper Sculptors' Tips and Tricks

MANY PAPER SCULPTORS are self-taught and have devised their own tricks and techniques. Hal Lose, for instance, sometimes uses a clothes steamer to relax paper enough to create complex curves. He assures a flawless finish to his work by smoothing the outer edge of each of his cuts with an etching tool. Dental tools are also part of Hal's paper sculpting toolbox; he often uses specially sharpened teeth-cleaning tools to score his papers.

Although some daring paper sculptors use a knife or blade as a drawing tool, at least on simple shapes, most use lightly drawn pencil lines as a guide to help them. Other sculptors tape photocopies of drawings or photographic reference material to their paper and cut through two layers of paper at once, eliminating the necessity of erasing pencil lines later on.

Many artists use pieces of foamcore to raise layers of paper, accentuate shadows, and give added dimension to works. The foamcore pieces are sometimes glued together to attain a height of as much as 4 inches

in works used for illustration and designed to be photographed head on. Other materials—such as four-ply matboard, foam tape, and even pieces of clear plastic—may also be used to elevate layers of a sculpture. When the sculpture is designed to be viewed from all angles, of course, elevating materials must be completely hidden.

Hidden attachments, used to glue sculpture elements to a heavy watercolor paper backing board or other support, include paper tabs and loops (like those created for a paper chain). White glue is applied to one side of the attachment and pressed against the backing while the other side is glued to the back of the sculpture piece.

Many sculptors have a favorite paper, but often the subject of the sculpture will dictate the paper to be used. David Wood works with BFK Reeves paper, using 250gsm for large work and 190gsm for smaller works. He finds it softer than watercolor paper and easier to manipulate. It embosses well, which is important when David chooses to add lines and textures to individual pieces.

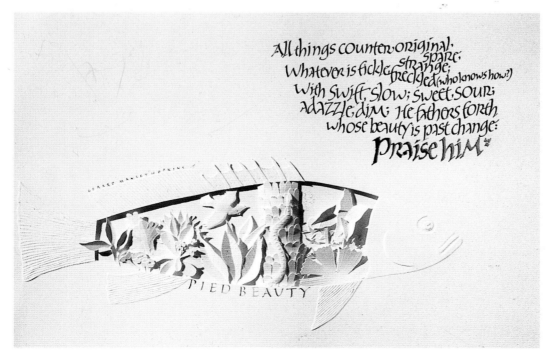

PIED BEAUTY BY DAVID WOOD
The intricate and delicate sculptures depicting the images in this poem have been inlaid behind the writing surface into the cut out shape of a fish.

Hal Lose likes to work on Canson Mi-Teintes and Canson Ingres papers, often marbling the paper to give another dimension to his work.

Nancy Cook prefers to work with Strathmore charcoal paper because "it's strong and forgiving" when you bend and crease it. She often uses charcoal paper to create a landscape, but switches to stiffer, stronger Arches watercolor paper in different weights to create other works that require a paper with more rigidity. Many of Nancy's paper sculptures, like *Pennsylvania Woodlands II*, feature very realistic-looking rocks. To create them Nancy uses a mottled Canson paper with a stiff "hand" to it. Because the paper is somewhat rigid, Nancy can cut a rock shaped piece of it, curve it, and then pinch it in a way that mimics the natural planes found on rocks in nature.

ABOVE *PENNSYLVANIA WOODLANDS II* BY NANCY LENORE COOK

RIGHT *IRISH WELCOME* (10 × 20 INCHES) BY NANCY LENORE COOK

A plate of fruit and vase of flower always greets Nancy when she visits a small hotel in Ireland. The joy she felt when seeing the familiar offering on her last trip inspired her to create this paper sculpture. She worked from a photograph and cut black paper to abstract the shape of the vase, its reflection, and shadow before adding more colorful detail to the piece.

A Paper-Sculpted Bird in Flight

THE FOLLOWING process steps describe how David Wood creates a simple structure of a bird in flight. David discovered a book called *Paper Sculpture* by Kathleen Ziegler and Nick Greco several years ago and "saw the vast possibilities of its use with calligraphy." His works now are a perfect marriage of the two mediums.

When starting a paper sculpture, David recommends that you either draw your own images or find a good photographic reference and make one photocopy to a size that can then be adapted to your specific needs.

David chose a bird in flight as his reference. He made a fine-line tracing of the bird to use for cutting out the individual pieces and also made one photocopy of the tracing to be used as a template for assembly later.

Since he is working with white paper, David makes sure his hands are clean before getting started. He cuts out the individual pieces by laying the tracing paper on top of his BFK Rives art paper. Using a new #11 blade in his knife, he cuts out individual pieces, allowing for an overlap so he has extra length to glue the pieces to one another.

The tracing of the bird from David Wood's *My Flight* and some of the paper pieces cut from a copy of the tracing.

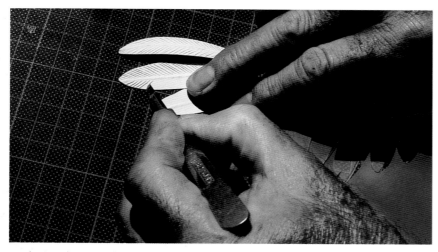

Feathering the scored bird feathers with a scalpel.

To create the feathers David cuts out each one individually and then scores it down the center with a stylus. To accomplish this, he takes a #15 curved scalpel blade and uses a process called "feathering," cutting halfway through the paper to create the "feathered look." He holds the scalpel at a shallow angle so the paper lifts.

Where the wings join the body, David thins the paper from the back with a very sharp scalpel blade. This reduces the thickness of the paper so that the join of the wings to the body is not so obvious when he glues the pieces together.

David cuts and glues one body part at a time—for example, wings, head, body, and so forth—so that pieces are not lost or damaged. This way, each section can be shaped individually on a thin plastic foam hobby mat (or padded placemat) by using a bone folder or a spoon burnisher.

David assembles all the parts of the bird with acid free PVA glue. He determines the distance the sculpture is to be raised from the background and uses small pieces of foamcore to create this dimension.

After assembly, David uses the feathering technique on the body to create the body feathers. If done at an earlier stage, he risks crushing them. He then completes the work by adding his calligraphic lettering.

ABOVE Thinning the paper where the wings join the body.
RIGHT Gluing the wing in place.

Elevating the bird's wing from its body with a piece of foamcore.

Creating the body feathers.

MY FLIGHT BY DAVID WOOD

A Pop-up Sculpture Garden

THE FOLLOWING demonstration describes how Nancy Cook creates a pop-up sculpture garden (page 94) which is a combination of collage, pop-ups, and paper sculpting techniques.

To create the garden walls, Nancy measures and cuts a piece of Canson paper to $8^1/_4 \times 8^3/_4$ inches. Then she draws a grid of intersecting lines on the paper $1^5/_8$ inches in from the paper's

edge. This becomes the interior of the garden. She uses a ruler and an awl to score the intersecting lines and valley-fold them, making it easier to later fold the walls and glue them together.

At this point, she cuts a $1^1/_2$-inch-wide opening in a short wall to receive a gate with parallel slits and horizontal cross bars that she had previously constructed. She next draws a stone pattern on the interior and exterior walls of the garden.

Before folding the corners of the garden into position, Nancy has to create a diagonal fold to allow the walls to be joined. Then she trims away the extra paper the diagonal fold creates so that only $^1/_4$-inch of paper borders each original grid line. Next she refolds the diagonal, and glues the $^1/_4$-inch paper overlaps at each corner to one another, thereby creating a walled structure. After the glue dries, she simultaneously pushes the sides of the garden down as she folds the front and the back of the garden walls flat. This creases the garden walls so that they can fold flat and pop-up again.

ABOVE Scoring the garden walls to begin folding them. RIGHT Folding the garden walls.

Next, Nancy cuts a $5 \times 5\frac{3}{8}$-inch "floor" for the garden and collages a brick pathway, as well as a rock bordered pond, onto it. She creates slits in the floor so that paper tabs extending from the base of flowers and bushes, cut from seed catalogs, can go through the slots beneath the floor and hold the foliage in place. She uses arch-shaped tabs of $\frac{1}{4}$-inch-wide strips of paper to join the plants to one another and to the sides of the garden walls. When the long sides of the garden are pushed toward the center and the short sides of the structure are folded down, these tabs cause the plants to fold, too. When all tabs are in position, she adheres the floor to the garden base.

To make the garden a lush and inviting place, Nancy glues multiple layers of paper-sculpted trees to the interior and exterior walls of the garden and adds a paper-sculpted garden bench. To make a tree, she draws and then cuts out the tree trunk and branches. Then she curves the paper with a bone folder to add strength to the shape.

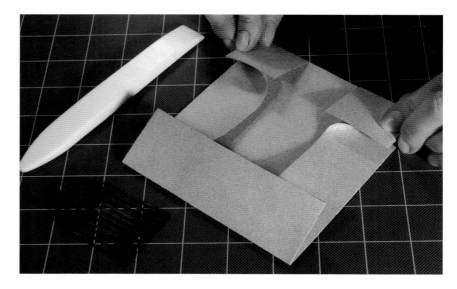

Gluing the garden walls together.

ABOVE Creasing and folding down the garden to create a pop-up design.
LEFT A side view of the completed garden.

Next she cuts out the leaf shapes and creates ruffled leaf edges keeping her scissor hand stationary as she turns the paper being cut. She uses a bone folder to add shape to the leaves and then glues the leaf shapes to one another with tiny V-folded tabs of paper. The tabs allow the leaves to float a bit to add dimension. Then she glues the leaves to the tree branches.

To create the garden base, Nancy cuts a $5^3/4 \times 6^1/4$-inch piece of matboard and covers it with grass-colored paper. She adds more bricks to the walkway to continue it outside the gate and places brown paper mulch beneath the trees to add more realism before finishing by finally adhering the garden to its base.

ABOVE Creating paper sculpture trees. Note how the base of the flat tree differs from the tree trunks shaped with a bone folder.

RIGHT *POP-UP SCULPTURE GARDEN* BY NANCY LENORE COOK The front view of the completed garden.

Gallery Tour

TOUCH THE EARTH
(760 × 570MM) BY DAVID WOOD
David used papier-mâché, scoring, and feathering techniques, as well as sculptured images of mountains, temple and trees to create this piece. His fine calligraphy and the subtle use of silver foil add finishing touches to a remarkable work.

ABOVE *THE SHELL SEEKER*
(12 × 24 INCHES) BY NANCY
LENORE COOK
This paper sculpture was
inspired by some photos
Nancy took of her daughter
in Maine. Nancy explained
that it differs from the more
detailed work that preceded
it in that it is more abstract,
just suggesting the setting. As
in all of her work, the sculpture tells a story—this one of
a child's fascination with the
ocean and its treasures.

RIGHT *RAINFOREST*
(1000 × 760MM) BY DAVID WOOD
The background paper and
all the images of the fanciful
rain forest were hand painted
before the sculptures were
rendered. The images were
eventually placed behind a
cutout panel to give the work
further dimension.

ABOVE *LEDA AND THE SWAN LEGENDS* (16 × 20 INCHES)
BY NANCY LENORE COOK

This sculpture is the center panel of a triptych, featuring Leda, Queen of Sparta, transformed into a swan by Zeus. The repeated swan shapes—at the bottom and top of the panel—add to the tapestry effect. They are positioned to reflect the fact that when swans mate for life, they touch beaks.

LEFT *SEA FEVER* (DETAIL) BY DAVID WOOD

The stark white paper used in this sculpture, inspired by a John Masefield poem, lets the viewer focus on the intricacy of the cut work on the sails, ropes, and ladders.

CHAPTER 5

Building
3-D PAPER STRUCTURES

MANY TYPES of dimensional paper works can be made and enjoyed as art, decorative accents, or functional objects. Elaborate baskets, eccentric boxes, outrageous lamps, and stunning decorative screens are increasingly being shown in fine craft shops, galleries, and art shows. When I ask about the work of a particular artist, I'm always amazed to learn how many people creating these structures are relatively new to the paper medium. The sophistication of the artwork would lead one to believe that each paper artist has been concentrating on a particular discipline for many years. But many of the artists are former painters, fiber artists, and even furniture makers who developed their composition and design sense in a totally different medium. Some artists took a workshop in three-dimensional paper structures just for fun and became smitten. Many traditional book artists and papermakers (like some you'll meet in this chapter) were also once content to create conventional books and sheets of paper until they discovered ways to adapt their skills and create three-dimensional paper forms. Once you begin working with paper, you too may find that paper has a way of captivating, inspiring, and inviting you to explore its many structural possibilities.

OPPOSITE *SUNRISE* BY JENNIFER MORROW WILSON
PHOTO BY KEN WOISARD

Dimensional Paper Weaving

MOST OF US learned the simple under/over tabby weave in elementary school. As you can see from Patti Hill's amazing baskets, paper weaving can be taken to a much higher level of sophistication. Even works as complex as Patti's, however, are still based on a simple woven pattern using upright strips (the warp) and weavers (the weft) to create designs. Once you learn the basics of basketmaking, you will be able to create baskets in various shapes and sizes by simply beginning on different shaped forms.

BIKER BABE BY PATTI QUINN HILL
Patti calls this basket her "self-portrait" and notes that it is about what she does when she is not weaving—riding her Harley-Davidson Heritage Softail Classic motorcycle. The curls in this basket represent the silver studs on her saddle, saddlebags, and motorcycle jacket.

CREATING A WOVEN BASKET

Patti provided the instructions for the woven basket project that follows. Don't be intimidated by the length of the project. As well as being an excellent artist, Patti is an excellent teacher; she has written the instructions with lots of hand-holding so that beginning paper weavers can feel secure creating their first basket. Although you could hand cut the strips for the project, a pasta machine with some attachments will make your work much easier. Moderately priced pasta machines are often used for making polymer clay structures and are sold through many craft stores as well as cooking shops.

1 Painting the paper
Before your start to paint your paper, try to visualize the inside and outside of your basket. You have six surfaces that need to be painted. One piece of paper will be painted on one side to become your outside uprights and painted on the other side to become your inside uprights. Another piece of paper will be painted on both sides to become your weavers, both outside and inside. Paint

both sides of your curl paper as well. The paper that Patti painted for the basket was all done with a sponge. To paint paper with a sponge, first spray the paper with water, then dip the sponge into the bronze paint and use a scrubbing motion to apply the paint. Then use a dabbing method to sponge layers of paint in copper and bronze metallic colors on top. The same technique was used to paint the turquoise color.

2 Finding a mold
The mold Patti used in this project comes from a set of four plastic bowls in different sizes made by Sterilite. It measures 4 × 8 inches (h × w). If the bowl you're working with has a rolled or tapered rim, cut it off to give the bowl straight sides.

3 Using a fettuccini cutter
To cut your strips of paper ¼-inch wide, choose the fettuccini setting on your pasta cutter. Attach the pasta cutter to the corner of a table. When using the pasta cutter, position your paper in the center of the blades,

WHAT YOU'LL NEED
140-pound Arches rough watercolor paper (20 × 30 inches)

2½ yards of waxed linen or other thick thread

#18 tapestry needle

Acrylic paints

Acrylic varnish

Hand-cranked pasta cutter

Mold

Pushpins

Ruler

Scissors

Small clips

White glue

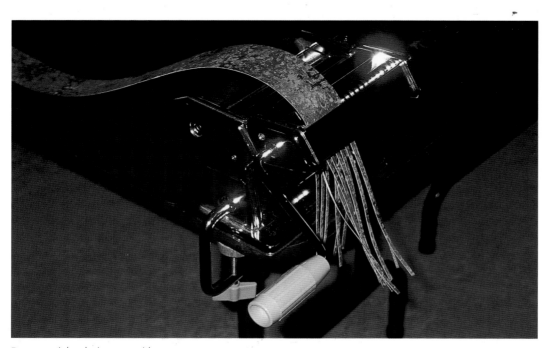

Paper uprights being cut with a pasta cutter.

dividing the waste on the edges evenly. Be sure the paper remains straight and unkinked as you feed it. Crank the handle a few turns at a time, looking under the pasta cutter and straightening out the paper, until it falls past the table edge. (*Note:* To avoid straining the cutter's gears, don't cut more than twelve strips of paper at a time.)

4 Creating the uprights

Cut twenty-two uprights, making them each 20 inches long and $^1/_4$-inch wide. To give you a few extras, and some wiggle room, use sheets of paper that are 7 inches wide.

TIP
To determine the length of uprights needed on any mold, measure from the top of the mold, down the side, across the bottom, up the opposite side, and around to the top of the mold. Add at least 4 more inches to this measurement to give you some weaving room when you take the basket off the mold.

The number of uprights used on any mold will vary depending on the mold and the weave structure used. For this project, you will use a twill weave structure. The base is woven with the uprights abutting one another. The bottom diameter of this mold measures 4 inches. To have the square woven base fit the round mold it will need to measure about 4 inches diagonally across the base. (The outer measurements of the base must be approximately 3 inches on all four sides, to give you approximately 4 inches across the base diagonally.) It will take eleven uprights, vertically woven over eleven uprights horizontally, to weave a base that measures 3 inches on all sides. I never figure this out mathematically. I just weave the base until it looks right and then see if it fits.

Insert 4 inches of paper (paper's full length: 30 inches) for uprights through the pasta cutter until you have cut the full length of the paper. Then insert 3 inches more paper through the pasta cutter. This will give you some extra. From this, cut twenty-two pieces at 20-inches-long each (or as wide and long as you need for your mold).

5 Laying out the base

Take two uprights and put a light pencil mark in the center of each one. Take one of these marked pieces and lay it on the table vertically. Place five pieces on either side of this center upright for a total of eleven vertical uprights making sure the edges line up. Place a heavy object on these pieces to keep them from moving.

Take the other piece marked in the center and begin weaving it horizontally at the center position of the eleven verticals starting with an "over two" weave. Continue to weave across these verticals, going under two, over two, etc., finally coming out the other side. Line up the center mark on this horizontal woven piece with the center mark of the vertical piece.

Now weave in the second horizontal piece starting at the right with an over one weave, and continue with under two, over two all the way across. Weave in the third piece starting at the right with under two, over two, under two, etc. Weave in the fourth piece starting at the right with under one, over two, under two, etc. You will notice a stair-stepping twill pattern stepping up toward the right. Weave in the fifth piece starting with over two. Weave in the last piece on this side starting with over one.

It is now safe to remove the weight that has been holding these vertical pieces in place. The weaving will hold it together. Turn the base 180 degrees and begin weaving five more pieces on the other side of the centerpiece, still stair-stepping to the right.

You should now have eleven uprights woven vertically, and eleven uprights woven horizontally. Count them to make sure. Check your stair steps for errors.

With the inside of the basket facing you, upset two uprights in each corner by folding the uprights along the edges of the woven base and creasing them. Place the inside of the basket against the mold and attach the woven base to the plastic mold with push-pins. Do not pierce the paper. Put the pins between the weaving into the mold.

6 Weaving up the sides

Cut the weaver paper into ⅛-inch-wide strips, using the trenette pasta cutter accessory. Cut them as you need them, doing a little at a time (Patti does 2 inches at a time) so as not to waste paper. Leave the weavers their full length (30 inches).

Put 2 inches of your weaver paper through the trenette cutter. Take one of these pieces and split it in half lengthwise with a knife or scissors to get two very

narrow pieces. Weave with these pieces first to start the sides. When you start weaving with your first weaver around the basket base, it will not be possible to follow the twill pattern completely around this first row.

Start in the upper left corner of the base weaving under two, over two, under two, etc. all the way around the base. When you get to each corner where you upset the uprights, try to move them together so that feet will begin to be formed. Stop when you get to your starting point.

In order to be able to weave continuously, you have to have an uneven number

TOP The basket base with upset uprights.
ABOVE The basket base attached to the mold with pushpins.

of uprights around the basket, so you will need to add an extra upright in this last corner. Take a $^1/_4$-inch-wide piece that is long enough to insert about 1 inch into the base weaving and be the same length as the rest of the uprights. Taper the end of this new upright for about 2 inches to give it a thin point. Insert the pointed end through the weaving into the base and then weave it as part of the basket in the twill pattern. This twill pattern will be stair-stepping up to the left. Weave with both pieces of narrow weavers, pulling in your corner uprights making the feet more pronounced. Also, start spreading the rest of the uprights evenly in a starburst fashion.

BELOW Splicing in a new narrow weaver to continue weaving up the sides.

BOTTOM Beginning the curls by clipping the curl piece on an under weave to secure it and wrapping the piece around clockwise.

To splice when you run out of weaver, end your weaver on an "over" set of two uprights. Take the new weaver, count back four sets of two uprights and place the weaver under two uprights to hide it. Weave on top of the ending weaver, proceeding over two, under two, spreading all of the uprights and rising up on the feet. Keep each row packed tightly to the row below, with no space between them. Make sure the uprights stay evenly spaced. *Note:* Do not weave tightly around the mold, just weave next to it; otherwise, the basket may be hard to remove.

7 Embellishing with curls

After you have woven the two narrow pieces, begin weaving with the trenette pieces ($^1/_8$-inch wide). Weave one row with a $^1/_8$-inch weaver and then start your curls. Curls are placed over each row as you weave.

Start your curl piece on an "under" weave and clip the strip to secure it. Wrap the piece around clockwise, making a small circle. Then place the curl piece behind the next under. Start with small curls and progress to larger curls as you weave up the mold and the basket gets larger. Use this same technique, making curls on top of (covering) all of your rows of weaving. All of the curls are done on an over and then secured behind an under. When you make a complete row of curls, you will return to the weaver piece. Drop the curl piece and pick up the weaver and weave another row around the basket. When you get back to the last curl that was made, drop the weaver and pick up the curl piece and continue to curl. As you progress up the side of the mold, remember to keep the uprights evenly spaced.

When you come to the end of your curl piece, you will need to splice a piece in to continue the curls. End your curl piece on an under and then splice on that same under by overlapping the pieces, making a double thickness. Put a clip on the splice to hold it securely until you get the next row of weaving in above it.

Continue weaving up to the top of the mold in this fashion, weaving a row, and placing a row of curls on top, covering it.

8 Removing the basket from the mold

Remove the pushpins and pull the basket off the mold.

Continue to weave and make curls. As you do this off the mold, the basket will begin to pull in on its own. Use the little clips to hold your weaving in place so it doesn't slip up.

Stop weaving whenever you desire, or until you have only ³/₄-inch of the uprights left. When you decide to stop, taper the end of your weaver for about 3 inches to a thin point. Trim down your curl piece to fit this taper.

Bend all of the uprights back and put a crease along the edge of the weaving. Make sure the uprights are standing straight up. Secure the weaving with clips.

Weave a ¹/₄-inch strip into these uprights. Proceed as before, going over two, under two, but *opposite* to your last row of weaving, not stair-stepping, but doing a plain weave. Use clips as you go along to hold this row in place. This is called the rim row. Make sure that this row of weaving is straight up.

Fold the uprights on the inside of the basket over the rim row and down. Cut these uprights just above the bottom of the rim row. Glue them to the rim row with a dot of white glue and secure with clips. Cut all of the uprights that are on the outside of the basket flush with the top of the rim row. Glue these uprights to the rim row and secure with clips until dry.

9 Attaching the rim

Decide which painted paper you want to use for your rims. True up the edge of the paper. Using scissors or an X-Acto knife, cut two rims 30 inches long and ³/₄-inch wide. It looks nice to use a couple of layers of different widths glued together on the outside rim.

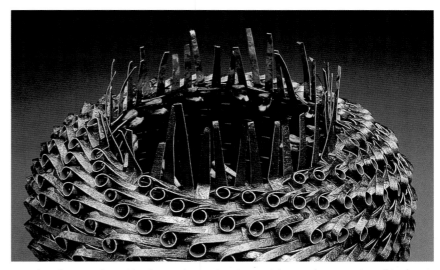
Securing the weaving with clips and creasing the uprights so they stand straight up.

The uprights glued to the rim row and secured with clips.

Overlapping and clipping the outside and inside rims in place to prepare for lashing.

Take one of the $^3/_4$-inch pieces that will be used for the inside rim, and cut off the corners giving the piece a flat point on the end. Place this point on the inside of the basket and clip it on the basket making sure that it does not go below the rim row. Clip snugly all the way around the basket. When you get to where you started, overlap behind this piece for about 2 inches, placing the point on top.

Start the outside rim on the same side of the basket as you started the inside rim. Place it just where the inside overlap ended. Clip snugly all the way around, flush with bottom of the last row of weaving.

When you get back to where you started, overlap for about 2 inches and put a flat point on the piece. Now both of the over-laps are on the same side of the basket. This is so that you will have room for adjustment at the end of the lashing. You can hold the rim a lot tighter with lashing than you can with clips.

10 Beginning the lashing

Thread the needle with the $2^1/_2$ yards of lashing thread to do single lashing (this is the amount needed for the basket). Start the lashing to the right of all of the over-laps. Thread your tapestry needle and take

TOP Beginning the lashing.
ABOVE The two lashing ends tied in a square knot.
RIGHT A detail shot of lashing and curls on the finished basket.

the long end tail of the thread and insert it, going upward between the inside of the basket and the inside rim. Do this in the space between the second and third uprights, to the right of the outside rim. Overlap on uprights that do not have curls. Pull the lashing up and over the top of the basket and insert the needle between the outside of the basket and the outside rim. Leave a 4-inch tail hanging down on the outside of the basket.

Bring the needle over to the outside of the basket and insert it into the basket between each upright, lashing around and around the rim. The long piece of thread and the needle will be coming from the outside to the inside of the basket. When you pull the thread, make sure to pull it straight out instead of up, so that you do not cut the paper rim with the thread. Pull very tightly all around the basket making

sure not to lose tension. Always insert the needle from the outside and pull the thread from the inside.

11 Ending and securing the lashing

When you get to where you started your lashing and all spaces between the uprights have been lashed, thread the tail that you left on the outside of the basket around an upright to the inside of the basket and tie the lashing ends in a square knot. Put a dot of glue over the knot to keep it from coming untied. When the glue dries, cut off the tail end pieces of the lashing.

12 Finishing

Use an acrylic varnish on the basket to stiffen it. Cut the varnish with two parts varnish to one part water, or use an acrylic spray varnish.

BELOW Two views of *Bronze Rhapsody*, the basket design Patti created for this project.

Papier-Mâché

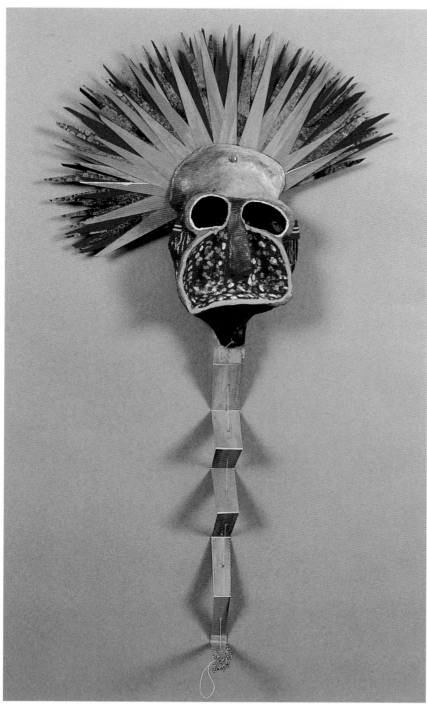

SAGE MASK BY SUSAN JOY SHARE
After painting her papier-mâché mask, Susan added collage work and an accordion-folded chin. The mask is almost 4 feet high.

PAPIER-MÂCHÉ, a French term meaning "chewed paper," was used in the eighteenth century to describe the process by which pulped paper and glue were transformed into various decorative objects. Although the French term persists, true papier-mâché actually began in China over a thousand years ago, when scraps of handmade paper were made into religious objects.

Papier-mâché is still used to produce religious and ceremonial pieces in Asian and Mexican cultures. In the United States, it is often used to create large, lightweight, theatrical costumes, as well as giant heads and masks to be worn in parades and carnivals.

There are two types of papier-mâché. One involves working with layers of paper and wallpaper paste; the other type involves working with Celluclay, a powdered paper pulp with a glue binder that handles like clay, and dries with a hard, slightly textured finish. The former method is considered the traditional one and, according to artist Linda Beazley, has the advantages of being quick-drying and of producing structures that are considerably smoother and lighter. This may not seem important in smaller works, but can be critical in larger ones.

Traditional papier-mâché involves coating strips of torn paper with diluted white glue or wallpaper paste. The dampened strips are then applied in multiple layers over removable molds such as bowls or vases, bases made from balloons or cardboard forms, or armatures constructed from wire, newspaper, and masking tape. Torn strips of newspaper or handmade paper can be used, as well as a finishing layer of decorative paper. Thin colored paper or tissue can be layered over a form and both the color and pattern can become a decorative focus in the work. Tearing, rather than cutting, paper will produce a papier-mâché work with a smooth, seamless finish.

THE CIRCUS ACT BY LINDA AND JOHN BEAZLEY
Because they tear, rather than cut them, the edges of the Beazley's paper strips fade from view and give their work an all-over smooth finish.

CREATING A PAPIER-MÂCHÉ ROOSTER

Linda and John Beazley favor the traditional papier-mâché method, which they use to create many wonderful creatures. They provided the following directions for making their papier-mâché rooster.

1 Creating the armature

To start the rooster form, wad two full-size sheets of newspaper into an oval shape to suggest the body of a bird and tape them securely together. Then shape a neck section, using one full sheet of newspaper. It should be about 7 inches in length, tapered near the head and made thicker where it joins the body. Tape the neck section tightly onto the body.

Next, you will make the rooster's legs. Cut a 15-inch-long piece of 18-gauge stovepipe wire for each leg and fold it in half. Twist the two sides around each other starting at the folded end. Near the bottom of the twisted leg, allow enough wire to form loops for the three-toed foot. Each leg should be about 7 inches long when

the twisting and forming is finished. Now attach the wire legs, one to each side of the oval body, and add a small amount of wadded paper to the area where the leg joins the body. Cover the wire legs with masking tape.

Make the large curved tail feathers from full-size sheets of paper. One thick and sturdy feather will act as a tripod to help the rooster balance and stand. Other feathers can be shaped with pipe cleaners. Twist pipe cleaners into a long loop, tape them to the body and then cover each loop with tape and arch it slightly. Four or five feathers make a good tail section.

For the rooster's head, form a small tight ball using a half-sheet of newspaper and tape it onto the tapered end of the rooster's neck. For the rooster's comb and beak, fold a sheet of newspaper about four times to establish a thick pad. Sketch out the shape of the comb, cut it out and tape it to the top of the rooster's head. The beak is a tiny cone made from a half-circle of folded newspaper.

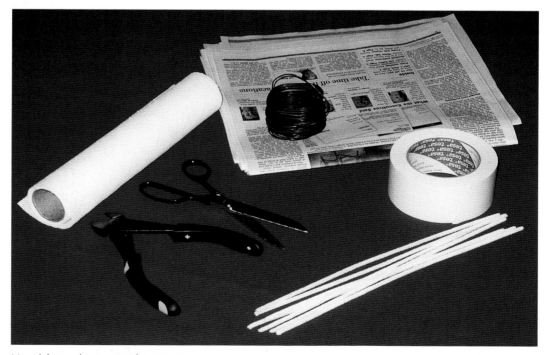

Materials used to create the rooster.

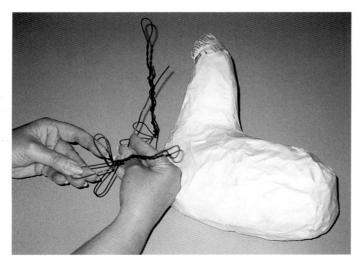

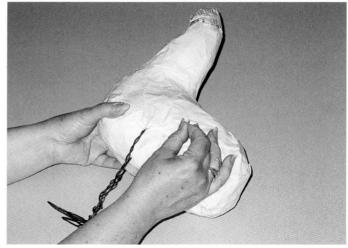

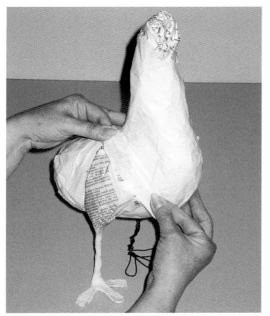

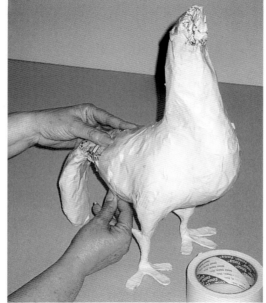

TOP LEFT Creating the wire legs to be added to the taped-newspaper rooster body.

TOP RIGHT Attaching the wire legs to the rooster body.

CENTER LEFT Covering the wire legs and remaining areas of the body with masking tape.

CENTER RIGHT Creating the tail section to help the rooster balance.

BOTTOM LEFT Attaching the rooster's head.

BOTTOM RIGHT Taping the beak onto the rooster's head.

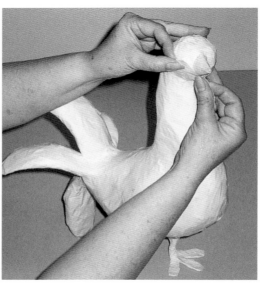

Tape it onto the rooster's head. The cock of the rooster's head is determined by the placement of the beak. The "wattle" (a loose skin section under the chin) is shaped like a large droplet of water. It is made from paper towels and taped into place.

Using half-sheets of newspaper, wad up a shape like a half-circle and tape it together to make wing parts. Make two of these and tape one to each side of the rooster. The rooster armature is now completed and covered in tape, ready to be cast in papier-mâché strips.

2 Casting the armature in papier-mâché

Tear small pieces of paper towels by hand (do not cut with scissors!). The torn edges

TOP LEFT Taping the wattle in place.
TOP RIGHT Taping a wing in place.
BOTTOM LEFT The rooster armature, ready to be cast in papier-mâché strips.
BOTTOM RIGHT Applying paste-soaked paper towel strips to the armature.

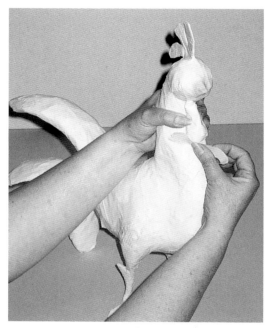

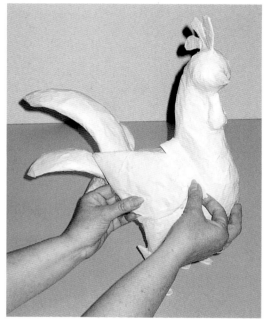

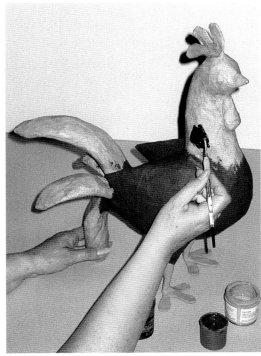

of paper towel blend together better for a smooth overall finished appearance. Dip each torn piece into liquid paste until saturated. (The Beazleys prefer commercial premixed wallpaper paste for its smooth, consistent texture.) Apply pieces individually to the rooster until the entire form is covered. Two layers or more provide a stronger surface. Allow the rooster to dry completely. This may take 2 to 4 hours, depending on the number of layers and the temperature of the environment.

3 Painting the finished piece

The rooster can be painted with acrylic or watercolor paints. The Beazleys often mix their own colors to obtain specific shades. Paints can be applied with brushes or sponges to achieve different effects.

4 Applying varnish

After painting the piece and letting the paint dry, apply a coating of satin varnish evenly with a brush. This step gives added protection and a slight sheen to the colors, making the vibrant rooster sculpture something to crow about.

Screens, Lamps, and Luminaries

THIN HANDMADE OR PURCHASED PAPER looks elegant and dramatic with light shining through it, which is one reason many paper artists are experimenting with creating screens, lamps, and luminaries as a way to show their paper work to advantage.

HINGED SCREENS AND FREESTANDING STRUCTURES

Panels of purchased or handmade paper can easily be connected to one another to create a tabletop screen or sculptural form. The hinges can be made of paper and patterned after an accordion-fold book so that the screen folds into several positions, to divide an area, conceal a surprise, or extend out in front of tea lights to show off the beauty of the paper. Hinges can also be made of metal jump rings, chain, leather, or ribbon.

Paper artist Claudia Lee creates her house panel screens from her handmade paper. Each panel is cut from a sheet of paper, handstitched using waxed linen

thread, and then folded in half and glued. The wrong side of the stitching is hidden inside each panel. The double-thickness panels create a strong heavy paper structure decorated with stitching on the front and back. The individual panels are then hand-stitched together in three to four places with waxed linen. Claudia explains how she became interested in creating the house structures: "The use of house forms goes back to my interest in how dwellings around the world are location appropriate in form and materials, and how they 'work' in their environment. I'm originally from New York City and the cityscape is my remembrance of that place. The text in the piece is from my grandmother's journal with a nod to graffiti, that great city art form. Stitching came naturally for me—I've been stitching on paper since I threaded yarn through punched cards as a kid. It was the natural choice to add color, pattern, and surface texture. It also adds to the story."

HOUSE PANEL SCREEN
BY CLAUDIA LEE
Claudia folds sheets of her handmade paper in half and stitches them to adjoining panels with waxed linen thread to create a strong paper screen.

Calligrapher Sharon Hanse artfully used brass wire to connect sections of her freestanding work *Rage*. She sandwiched vertical wires with curled ends between the layers of each of the five sides of her work, making a place for the wires to attach and create a hinge. The wires were flattened with a hammer, the curled to create a pattern.

The large 20 × 36-inch sculptural floor screen shown on page 116 is a collaborative work by paper artist Jennifer Morrow Wilson and her metalsmith husband, Douglas Wilson. The combination of vivid collaged and stitched paper, and forged steel echoing the paper shapes, creates a dramatic structure, with or without illumination.

RAGE BY SHARON LEE HANSE
Although more a sculpture than a screen, it too can be opened and repositioned to assume a different shape.

SCREEN BY JENNIFER MORROW WILSON AND DOUGLAS WILSON
The front of the scupltural floor screen (top) and the back (bottom). Photo by Ken Woisard.

Jennifer explained that the concept for the piece came from the natural environment of rocky shore and evergreen forest in which they live. She described the collaborative process: "We sketched out ideas together, and Doug forged the framework and wave elements. I made paper panels to fit the frames, leaving a margin to sandwich the paper between the front and back of the frames. Since it is a two-sided piece, I have worked both surfaces with collage, drawing, stenciling, and stitching."

LAMPS AND LUMINARIES

Exciting large and small functional lamps and nightlights can be made by illuminating a paper structure.

Sometimes artists can be inspired by a traditional design and then alter it to create a unique structure that reflects their own personality. Claudia Lee used a popular origami pattern to create a box with pleated sides and a foldover flap as a starting point to begin designing her charming batiked night lights. Then she cleverly outfitted them with paper-covered wooden legs and added a screen-covered bottom section. The screen holds the base open and allows the heat and additional light from a nightlight inserted in the back of the lamp to disperse. The fanciful handmade and hand-decorated papers she created for the lights are accented with stitching.

Batiked paper lamps by Claudia Lee.

Jennifer Morrow Wilson's lamps also feature stitching. She creates a kind of quilt out of her handmade paper pieces to create colorful and glowing table lamps. When they are illuminated, light shines through the many stitching holes, creating many dramatic points of light. Jennifer describes her work *Sunrise* (see page 98): "*Sunrise* explores the transmission of light through translucent paper and pierced holes. It uses the traditional textile techniques of piecing and stitching with the alternative materials or paper and metal screening. The change between unlit and lit states is important to me—that 'aha' moment when the paper is transformed through light."

Papermaker Helen Hiebert creates beautiful luminaries featuring watermarked designs. To create the designs, she cuts images, such as leaves, out of adhesive-backed rubber and adheres them to her papermaking mold. The pulp remains thinner over the raised designs and creates

ABOVE *PIECED TABLE LAMP* BY JENNIFER MORROW WILSON
Jennifer's lamp, made of pierced handmade and commercial papers, takes on a new personality when illuminated. Photo by Ken Woisard.

RIGHT *AUTUMN LEAF LUMINARIA* BY HELEN HIEBERT
A wooden base holds Helen's watermarked handmade paper in place and preserves its square shape.

a watermark, which allows more light to come through. The simple square paper structures are supported by wooden bases that Helen designs and builds.

Barbara Fletcher creates whimsical lamps by first constructing a wire screen armature and then spraying it with wet paper pulp blown out of a spray gun at high pressure. Her lamps may take the form of fantasy creatures, animals, and fish or more conventional lampshade structures. After the blown pulp is dry, Barbara colors her pieces with dyes and acrylics to give them the luminescent quality for which they are known. Then the paper form is placed over a regular lampshade that is used to support the handmade sculpture. Barbara makes air vents in the purchased shade to disperse the heat and often balances the handmade shade with tiny weights. She fits her lamps with low wattage bulbs to avoid overheating the paper.

Pulp-sprayed lamps by Barbara Fletcher.

Decorative Boxes

PIECES OF BOOKBOARD or heavy matboard can be glued to one another to create a functional box. When covered in decorative paper and capped with a collaged lid, a utilitarian box can be changed into a work of art. Because no one can resist sneaking a peek inside a box, you might add additional decoration there or add interest to the side walls by adorning them with collage-covered bookboard panels in descending sizes. Square or rectangular boxes are easiest to make, but as you gain experience, you can angle the corners where walls join and create boxes with triangular and even hexagonal shapes.

COVERED BOX BY RUTH ANN PETREE
An assortment of papers combined with beads, ribbons, and collage elements gives a unique personality to each of Ruth Ann's boxes.

Ruth Ann Petree's exquisite boxes are featured in many collections. She has created work for special clients through her business Quasivecchio, including pieces for *Oprah* and *Better Homes and Gardens*. Ruth Ann often decorates her boxes inside and out with collage work, ribbons, and beads, making them seem more like assemblage art than useful containers. She provided the following instructions for creating a rigid box and alternative lids.

1 Covering a piece of bookboard

Determine the size of your box—its width, length, and height. Select a piece of bookboard large enough to accommodate cutting out the sides and box bottom. Match board and paper grain (marking the bookboard to keep track of the grain), and using dry adhesive, adhesive spray or PVA (polyvinyl acetate) adhesive, cover the piece of bookboard with the black paper. (*Note:* Ruth Ann says she sometimes paints the bookboard with black acrylic paint rather than covering it with black paper or leather.) Press the board and paper covering overnight if using PVA. Note the board grain again before proceeding, keeping in mind that for this project, the grain of the bookboard and that of the decorative paper covering the exterior of the box should run parallel to the box wall length.

2 Cutting out the box pieces

Cut the base to reflect the length and width dimensions of the box. Cut two sides—the width of the box, by the height of the box. Cut another two sides—the length of the box, plus two board thicknesses, by the height of the box.

3 Assembling the box

Assemble the box by brushing adhesive along the wall edges where they meet the base board and each other. Glue up one board at a time and use masking tape to hold outside the corners together until the adhesive sets, if necessary.

4 Covering the box sides

This method uses one continuous piece of decorative paper to cover the outside and overlap the interior of the box and the box base by a $1/2$-inch. The length of the paper should be twice the length of the box plus twice the width of the box, plus four board thicknesses, plus a $1/2$-inch. The width of the paper should be the height of a box wall, plus 1 inch plus one board thickness.

On the wrong side of this paper, score a $1/2$-inch margin down the left side and along the lower edge. Gently fold along the score lines, then apply PVA adhesive (to the boards rather than on the paper) as follows.

WHAT YOU'LL NEED

Bookboard or heavy matboard

Black foam sheeting for box base and lid liner (Ruth Ann recommends Darice for foam sheeting)

Black paper for lining the bookboard

Bone folder

Box support (optional)

Decorative paper for covering the box

Masking tape

Matboard and ribbon for box lid decoration

Mat knife or heavy-duty board cutter

Pencil

PVA glue

Small and large glue brushes

Steel square

The black-paper-lined box walls and bottom, ready to be assembled.

The box, with one wall glued in place, on the scored paper.

Brush the adhesive mixture on the outside of one side wall of the box. Set it in place along the scored lines of the paste paper. Press the decorative paper against the box wall. Place a clean paper over the paste paper and smooth the decorative paper down with a bone folder. Work in the direction of the grain to avoid stretching it. Continue this process one wall at a time. To avoid air bubbles, work the decorative paper around each corner by pulling it with one hand and pressing it to the box wall with the other. For the last wall, brush adhesive on the entire wall and press down the 1/2-inch flap. Brush adhesive lightly onto the edge of the paper that overlaps this flap. Pull the paper around the corner and smooth the last wall's covering into place. Be sure to go around the box frequently to smooth the wall covering with your bone folder.

RIGHT Mitering the paper corners on the box base. BELOW Folding the decorative paper over the top of the box walls.

To miter the outside corners of the box base, hold the box upside down or prop it up by placing it over a support. Pinch the excess paper together. Hold your scissors parallel to the box bottom as shown below. Keep enough paper at the corner point to cover the base board and then clip off the excess. Adhere edges in place with adhesive.

5 Bringing the paper over to the inside of the box

The following easy method of cutting a slit in the paper used to fold over the box walls will work with small boxes. Larger boxes may require the use of a triangle to determine the size of the triangular-shaped slit.

Turn the box right side up and at each corner cut a very narrow triangular-shaped slit down to the top of the box. This cutaway slit should not be wider than the board thickness.

6 Pasting down the foldovers

Begin pasting the foldovers on the short walls first—one wall at a time. Brush adhesive on the 1/2-inch flap of paper at one side of the box. Pull the lining over the top edge of the box and press and rub with a bone folder. Pull the lining to the inside of the box and press it against the inside wall. Smooth it in place with a bone folder. Continue at each side until all of the box walls are lined with the narrow foldover of decorative paper.

7 Covering the box base

Adhere a covering material to the outside of the box base made from black paper or black foam slightly smaller than the box base—about 1/8-inch smaller all around. Press it down with your fingers and then smooth with a bone folder.

8 Creating the lid

The lid consists of two parts with a foam lid liner (1/8-inch smaller than the box opening) resting inside the box to keep the lid in place. One of Ruth Ann's lids is 1 inch larger in length and width than her box bottom, which creates a lid with a $1/2$-inch overhang. She has covered it with decorative paste paper and created a two-part central panel featuring an abstract painting glued down over four flat African beads. The second lid, which also features a foam liner that fits the box, is rectangular in format with a decorated central panel featuring a reproduction from an ancient manuscript. Two layers of ribbon passing through holes punched in the panel are joined with a bead.

Create a lid according to your wishes. This is the place to get really creative! Cover your lid with decorative paper using the directions for covering the accordion-fold book boards. Then add beads, ribbons, or panels to transform a rather plain box into an extraordinary container.

Ruth Ann's finished box with its ribbon-decorated lid.

The completed paste-paper covered box with a lid featuring an abstract painting and four flat African beads.

Gallery Tour

JACK LAMP (24 × 11 × 11 INCHES)
BY HELEN HIEBERT

By manipulating a couched sheet of paper and letting it dry over a form, Helen created a wildly abstract handmade paper shade. The lamp pictured is one in a series of lamps Helen created using found objects as bases. Photo by James Dee.

GUINEA HEN, CURLY QUATREFOIL PLATTER, BLACK-EYED PEARL, AND *MICACEOUS OVAL* BY PATTI QUINN HILL
These dimensional paper weavings from Patti's "Black and White Series" were inspired by the pearl guinea hens she keeps on her farm. Patti is able to create vessels in most any shape and size. *Guinea Hen*, the tall black vessel shown here, is 14 × 10½ inches.

FISH LAMPS BY BARBARA FLETCHER
To give her delightfully humorous fish lamps colorful and realistic body patterns, Barbara combines batik and stencil techniques with luminiscent dyes. Photo by Jan Bindes.

MANUFACTURERS AND WHOLESALE DISTRIBUTORS

Listed here are the manufacturers and wholesale suppliers for many of the materials used in this book. These companies sell their products to retailers of paper arts supplies. Your local retailer's knowledgeable personnel can advise you on your purchases, and if you need something they don't have in stock they will usually order it for you. If you can't find a store in your area that carries a particular item or will accept a request for an order, or if you need special assistance, a manufacturer will gladly direct you to the retailer nearest you that carries their products and will try to answer any other questions you might have.

Arnold Grummer Papermaking
316 N. Milwaukee St.
Milwaukee, WI 53202
800-453-1485
www.arnoldgrummer.com
Papermaking supplies

The C-Thru® Ruler Co.
6 Britton Dr.
Bloomfield, CT 06002
800-243-8419
www.cthruruler.com
Metal-edged rulers

Carriage House Paper
79 Guernsey St.
Brooklyn, NY 11222
800-669-8781
www.carriagehousepaper.com
Papermaking supplies

Diane Maurer Hand Marbled
Papers
P.O. Box 78
Spring Mills, PA 16875
814-422-8651
www.dianemaurer.com
Decorative papers

Dieu Donné Papermill
433 Broome St.
New York, NY 10013
212-226-0573
www.dieudonne.org
Papermaking supplies, paper

FURTHER READING

Barton, Carol. *The Pocket Paper Engineer.* Glen Echo, Maryland: Popular Kinetics Press, 2005.

Carter, David A. and James Diaz. *The Elements of Pop-Up.* New York: Little Simon, 1999.

Chatani, Masahiro. *Pop-Up Gift Cards.* Tokyo: Ondorisha Publishers, Ltd, 1988.

Dawson, Sophie. *The Art and Craft of Papermaking.* Philadelphia: Running Press, 1992.

Heller, Jules. *Papermaking.* New York: Watson-Guptill Publications, 1997.

Hiebert, Helen. *The Papermaker's Companion.* Pownal, VT: Storey Books, 2000.

———. *Paper Illuminated.* Pownal, Vermont: Storey Books, 2001.

Johnson, Pauline. *Creative Bookbinding.* New York: Dover, 1990.

Kaar, Joan B. *Paper Making and Bookbinding, Coastal Inspirations.* East Sussex, England: Guild of Master Craftsman Publications Ltd., 2003.

Lee, Claudia K. *Papermaking.* New York: Lark Books, 2001.

Maurer-Mathison, Diane. *The Art and Craft of Handmade Cards.* New York: Watson-Guptill Publications, 2003.

Siliakus, Ingrid. *Origamic Architecture from Building to Card.* Baarn, Holland: Cantecleer, 2002.

Webberley, Marilyn and JoAn Forsyth. *Books, Boxes and Wraps: Bindings and Building Step-by-Step.* Kirkland, Washington: Bifocal Publishing, 1995.

Ziegler, Kathleen and Nick Greco. *Paper Sculpture.* Rockport, Massachusetts: Quarry Books, 1996.

CONTRIBUTORS

Carol Barton
Glen Echo, MD
cbarton@mindspring.com
www.popularkinetics.com

Linda and John Beazley
Pottstown, PA
LSBZ23@aol.com

Lynne Carnes
Tucson, AZ
www.PaperPortals.com

Nancy Lenore Cook
Trappe, MD
Scheren@chesapeake.net

Anne-Claude Cotty
Stonington, ME

Constance Dawley
Longview, WA

Leslie Ebert
Portland, OR
www.LeslieEbert.com

Daniel Essig
Asheville, NC
www.danielessig.com
dessignc@earthlink.net

Barbara Fletcher
Billerica, MA
www.paperdimensions.com
Barbara@paperdimensions.com

Debra Glanz
Portland, OR
www.reminiscencepapers.com
Debra@reminiscencepapers.com

Sharon Lee Hanse
Barnesville, OH
www.toucancalligraphy.com
Hanse@1st.net

Helen Hiebert
Portland, OR
www.enlightenedpapers.com
Helen@enlightenedpapers.com

Patti Quinn Hill
Weaverville, NC
Pattiquinnhill@charter.net

Mary Howe
Stonington, ME
Mch@media2.hypernet.com

Sandy Jackson
Seattle, WA
www.some-assembly-required.com
Sandy@some-assembly-required.com

Joanne B. Kaar
Caithness, Scotland
www.joannebkaar.com
Info@joannebkaar.com

Anne Kenyon
State College, PA

Claudia Lee
Liberty, TN
Paperlee@dtccom.net

Hal Lose
Philadelphia, PA

Joan B. Machinchick
Arnold, MD
Lakeclaire@toad.net

Jeffery Mathison
Spring Mills, PA
www.artbymathison.com

Paul Maurer
Serafina, NM

Betsy R. Miraglia
Bryn Mawr, PA
Paperfly1@aol.com

Fred B. Mullett
Seattle, WA
www.fredbmullett.com
Fredb@fredbmullett.com

Ruth Ann Petree
Portsmouth, RI
Quasivecchio@cox.net

Jeanne Petrosky
St. Peters, PA
www.jeannepetrosky.com

Jennifer Philippoff
Rebersburg, PA
Joynglee@yahoo.com

Susan J. Share
Anchorage, AK
Sjshare@compuserve.com

Ingrid Siliakus
Amsterdam, Holland
http://members.chello.nl/rebran/

Sandy Stern
Glenwood, MD

Marjorie Tomchuk
New Canaan, CT
www.Mtomchuk.com
MTomchuk@aol.com

Jennifer Morrow Wilson
Little Deer Isle, ME
www.morrowwilsonstudios.com
Jmorrowwilson@acadia.net

David Wood
Surf Beach, Australia
www.davewood.com.au
Info@davewood.com.au

INDEX